on track ...

David Bowie

1964-1982

every album, every song

Carl Ewens

sonicbondpublishing.com

Sonicbond Publishing Limited
www.sonicbondpublishing.co.uk
Email: info@sonicbondpublishing.co.uk

First Published in the United Kingdom 2024
First Published in the United States 2024

British Library Cataloguing in Publication Data:
A Catalogue record for this book is available from the British Library

ISBN 978-1-78952-324-9

Typeset in ITC Garamond Std & ITC Avant Garde Gothic
Printed and bound in England

Graphic design and typesetting: Full Moon Media

Follow us on social media:
Twitter: https://twitter.com/SonicbondP
Instagram: www.instagram.com/sonicbondpublishing_/
Facebook: www.facebook.com/SonicbondPublishing/

Linktree QR code:

Acknowledgements

I would like to thank my good friend Gavin Fuller for his tireless comments on all things musical and also for his particular take on Bowie's *Diamond Dogs* period. Also, I'd like to thank my eldest, Keira and her partner, Jack Bliss, for their discussion and interest in the project. Thanks as well to 'Ser Eliot of Sussex', our middle child, who had to sit through endless hours of his dad's favourite Bowie albums on car journeys, jotting down notes. And my felicitations go out to our youngest, Dylan, for putting up with my random music-related musings, and most of all to my beautiful wife Beverley, for her fantastic forbearance and support throughout this book's gestation.

Thanks are also due to Stephen Lambe, who originally accepted this book for publication as part of the hallowed *On Track* series. He is very helpful and patient.

I'd like to thank work colleagues Eleanor Harrison, Andrea Bailey, Kev Chapell and Tim Moyse for their having to listen to me waffle on about Bowie so much. Also, Nick Bennet for having a look at the *Aladdin Sane* chapter for me and giving me the thumbs-up, saying, 'I found out things I didn't know about Bowie. I'd buy it.'

Finally, I'd like to thank Joe Frost – my best friend and musical collaborator of many years – for advice, interest and insight.

I believe there is an energy form.

The bedrock of my spirituality is Buddhism and Nietzsche: impermanence, transience – nothing is going to stay around very long. Everything changes.

I do have a very strong belief in a force. There is something else other than us. That's as near as I can get to it. It may just be people on other planets that I'm thinking about; it may be God. There is a definite force that I feel.

David Bowie, from the film *Moonage Daydream* (2022)

on track ...
David Bowie
1964-1982

Contents

Introduction

And in the death
As the last few corpses lay rotting in the slimy thoroughfares
The shutters lifted an inch in temperance building, high on
Poachers Hill and red mutant eyes gazed down on Hunger City
No more big wheels
Fleas the size of rats sucked on rats the size of cats
And ten thousand peopleoids split into tribes
Coveting the highest of the sterile skyscrapers.
'Future Legend' 1974

Bowie's childhood friend Geoff McCormack recalls that when they were young, David used to love gruesome horror stories. He used to like the effect that monsters and supernatural stories had on people. This would prove to be a very great insight into Bowie's personality. Later in his career, there were several songs and albums showing this influence of the eerie and sinister in his songwriting.

Another major influence on Bowie's development as a person was his father's work as a publicity officer for the children's charity Dr Barnardo's. During charity shows, David's dad Haywood Stenton Jones (known as John) introduced his wide-eyed son to the many stars of the day in the UK, getting their autographs and developing a definitive focus on the performers' costumes, the fans, the glamour, but probably above all, the music – the sheer spectacle of the entertainer.

Another even more telling influence on much of Bowie's music was his older half-brother, Terry Burns. Turning him on to the beat poets and writers like Burroughs, Ginsburg and Kerouac, current trends in art and music, and especially cool jazz artists like John Coltrane, Ornette Coleman and Miles Davis, Terry was as much a living representative of the beatnik generation as his brother. Another side of this intense brotherly relationship was Terry's eventual descent into mental illness, triggered by experiences in the Royal Air Force and his troubled family background. (As Peggy's illegitimate child, he was only grudgingly allowed at the family home, his step-father having little time for him).

The beginning of David's musical evolution was as much in jazz as in early rock 'n' roll, with John Coltrane vying with Little Richard for attention. David was as much taken with the saxophone players in Little Richard Penniman's backing band as he was with their exorbitant singer. When he started his musical career, it was as a sax player, and it was only later, when the flaky lead singer in his after-school band The Kon-Rads failed to appear, that he took over on vocals.

Bowie played for a series of mod bands throughout the 1960s but ended up being stopped in his tracks by the hippie counterculture and – counterintuitively – popular middle-of-the-road comedy entertainer and

9

singer Anthony Newley. This was part of David's genius; he could be simultaneously into the subculture and overtly cheesy Middle England at the same time. Both the subculture and the culture at large had a strong pull on David's nature, giving him the ability to create art that was at once distinctive and crowd-pleasing. It's also important to note that this clash of sensibilities led to an unholy alliance between the two sides of his personality – the curiosity about the arcane and the outsider – and a dalliance with commercial art and public image. In fact, it is a salutary point to remember that as a young man in London, he worked – albeit for a short time – in an advertising agency as a junior visualiser. There, he would've no doubt become aware of standard advertising ploys and ideas about the marketing of a product while disabusing himself of any illusion about the nine-to-five working life. His head was turned by the wilder side of the drug-fuelled nightlife of the capital and its more-industry-oriented machinations, and he was ever-after in thrall to an all-consuming desire to create art first and foremost.

With his first album, there was a mountain of songs to choose from – many created from a desire to write hits for other pop artists, as well as songs for a possible stage musical. The chapter that covers Bowie's first album is easily the longest in this book because Bowie turned his hand to all kinds of songs with the mistaken idea that he would become some sort of jobbing songwriter. Weirdly, this was exactly what two of his future collaborators *did* become – Lou Reed and Ian Hunter worked for a while with music publishers to produce commercial pop songs in the late 1960s.

With the persona Bowie created for the first album being solidly presented as an all-round entertainer, he was positioning himself for a career in a certain mould, emulating his then-idol Newley. This cheeky-chappie, lovable, cockney singer-songwriter failed to ignite the pop world, unless you count Bowie's later hit 'The Laughing Gnome' – re-released by his former record company Deram to cash in on his arrival as Ziggy, in the 1970s. This was the albatross that Bowie wore around his neck for the rest of his career.

When the debut Deram solo album failed, manager Ken Pitt helped Bowie move on and continue plugging away with his multifaceted talent, including stints as an actor and a mime artist (supporting his friend Marc Bolan's psych-folk group Tyrannosaurus Rex). He also had a residency playing gigs at the old Marquee club on Wardour Street, renamed for his performances there – these Marquee nights were titled The Bowie Showboat, as Pitt still wanted to present Bowie as an all-round entertainer – which allowed him to build a dedicated following among kids and the cognoscenti.

Bowie's songwriting took some strange twists as he tried to find fame, the next step in his development being a move towards a more folk-orientated approach, softening his vocal style to some degree and working with other players in a group called Feathers: with his girlfriend Hermione Farthingale, and a second guitarist John Hutchinson from the north of England.

Whilst preparing material for a follow-up album, David began writing in a variety of styles, including topical songs related to hippy 'happenings' or other groovy 'scenes' that were going on around town and observational songs and skits. A number of these can be heard in a box set called *Conversation Piece*, discussed in the last section of this book. He took part in the Beckenham Arts Lab (basically a folk club above a pub), where he not only performed himself but invited many luminaries of the late-1960s to play. This culminated in his next album's psychedelic closing track, 'Memory Of A Free Festival', with its closing chant, 'The sun machine is coming down, and we're gonna have a party'.

Bowie finally hit pay dirt with 'Space Oddity', and though this sudden success was a big boost to his ego and a welcome relief from being a commercial failure, it proved to be somewhat of a false dawn. Somehow intuiting the forthcoming success of his friend Marc Bolan's band T.Rex, who had recently gone electric and become more pop-oriented, he'd talked Bolan into playing lead guitar on the follow-up single 'The Prettiest Star'. This began another period of flop singles for Bowie, lasting until 1972. However, it was during this period that David's songwriting really took off and he began to write epics like 'Cygnet Committee', very much in the mode of the previous era's defining artist Bob Dylan; Bowie eventually bidding to steal the Hibbing bard's mantle with 'Song For Bob Dylan' on 1971's *Hunky Dory*.

Finally, Bowie achieved career liftoff in 1972 with 'Starman' and its parent album *The Rise And Fall Of Ziggy Stardust And The Spiders From Mars*. His Ziggy Stardust persona became synonymous with David himself, although perhaps originally conceived as just a character in what amounted to another attempt at writing that coveted stage musical, with that memorable career-defining moment when Bowie put the part to bed at the final gig as Ziggy, at the Hammersmith Odeon in 1973 (see Live Albums section). He went on to create character after character, which gave him other perspectives to sing from – the next being Aladdin Sane, who reflected a fuller acquaintance with the original land of rock 'n' roll: the huge amorphous entity known as the US. In the song 'Cracked Actor', Bowie sang from the perspective of an old film star, and in 'Panic In Detroit', from that of an urban terrorist. But these were all part of his own personal quest for an understanding of what drove him to create, to make art, to love life, and to understand the motivations of others.

Next, he was involved in a doomed attempt to create a real stage musical, this time based on George Orwell's dystopian 20th-century masterpiece *1984*. Though the musical didn't come to pass, it fired David's imagination to create sets and costumes which were all used in the tour promoting the album *Diamond Dogs* – his *own* version of a dystopian future, set in the fictional post-apocalyptic Hunger City, where his new character Halloween Jack led a mutant gang. The show was superbly staged, put together with extreme care, and was ambitious for its time, touring the US to great acclaim, the set

11

designs for Hunger City being atmospheric and affecting. It is a great pity that it was not filmed: only fragments of video survive.

When the urge came to truly immerse himself in the soul of America, Bowie was led to Philadelphia, coincidentally where his great *David Live* album was recorded. The album captured the rich, emotional music played by a very adept band, slowly morphing from rock into soul, with the end product being *Young Americans*: Bowie's breakthrough album in the US. Full of beautifully produced music, with *The Man Who Sold The World* producer Tony Visconti back on board, *Young Americans* was a true career watershed as Bowie reinvented himself yet again. This time, there was no new character as such, and perhaps some of these songs really are, to some degree, confessional, giving a true insight into this sensuous and delicate musician, singer, writer and performer.

Unfortunately, Bowie had become embroiled in the rock-world drug culture on the US tour, and when he moved to Los Angeles in order to consider his next step, the habit he'd taken up threatened to derail him. Cocaine was the drug of choice then: a substance known to inflate the ego and induce delusions of grandeur. Bowie's appearance on *The Dick Cavett Show* showed him conspicuously sniffing and twitching, enigmatically carrying a cane, and speaking in a boisterous and conspiratorial way, his host bemused and perhaps concerned.

The album Bowie made around this time – conceived in a drugged haze – was one of his most exotic creations: *Station To Station*. If ever an album sought to take on big themes, to engage with unusual and arcane notions, this was it. Like Dylan's trilogy of 1970s albums that began with *Blood On The Tracks*, *Station To Station* is a document of a singular obsessive mind, not merely interested in songs relating to human relationships but in wider, more spiritual themes. The music was the most sublime melding of wild guitar overdrive from new right-hand men Earl Slick and Carlos Alomar, with funk and soul rhythms from bassist George Murray and drummer Dennis Davis. Bowie's voice was supple and honed, with lyrics reflecting an interest in the arcane, the spiritual, futuristic technology, and love in all its forms.

Claiming to remember little from the sessions for that album, Bowie was rapidly becoming more and more excessive and deluded, with a palpable drug psychosis imbuing his latest persona, The Thin White Duke, and an unfortunate Nazi tinge, making remarks in contemporary interviews, such as that right-wing dictators might be a good idea. His mental health must have been in doubt. What saved Bowie from this life of lunacy was probably a strong grip on his spiritual beliefs (a song like 'Word On A Wing' was possible evidence of this), as well as his friendship with Iggy Pop. That relationship with Iggy – who had even worse drug problems – perhaps pulled Bowie up sharply, and in an attempt to get them both clean, they got together and moved first to France and then Berlin: a city and a culture that had long fascinated David.

Another watershed moment was his first feature film – an adaptation of Walter Tevis' iconoclastic science-fiction novel *The Man Who Fell To Earth*. Bowie strongly identified with the hero of the story, Thomas Jerome Newton, an alien who had come to Earth in desperation to save his home world, which was struggling with an eco-catastrophe. Its people sent their interplanetary pilgrim (played by David) to find resources to stabilise their planet. This put David into a solitary existence for some time in the southern desert of New Mexico, where he may have felt quite isolated. It inspired him to produce some odd music with 'Space Oddity' arranger Paul Buckmaster, which started Bowie trying to create strange alien music that reflected the desert terrain and something of his identification with the alien hero of director Nic Roeg's movie. Unfortunately, Roeg rejected Bowie's instrumental music but ignited Bowie's creative mind to think about maybe making an album of new music in this style.

When he and Jimmy Osterberg (Iggy) eventually hit the recording studio in France, Bowie was certainly fired up, and he ended up producing a number of albums (two of his own and two with Iggy), beginning at the Château d'Hérouville in France, but completed – as legend tells – in Hansa Tonstudios, Berlin, by the wall. *Low* and *"Heroes"*, along with Bowie's album *Lodger*, which seems to be included even though it was made in Switzerland, are known as Bowie's Berlin period.

His drug-taking was now less intense, though he'd taken to drinking in the bars of Berlin and was certainly no saint. He took to frequenting a gay bar and had an intense friendship with trans nightclub owner Romy Haag, living in a roomy but faceless apartment in Hauptstrasse with Iggy and personal assistant Corrinne Schwab. He and Iggy were not averse to the many pleasures, via the bierkellers and discotheques that Berlin's nightlife had to offer. But the work he did there with Iggy, ambient composer Brian Eno and faithful ally Tony Visconti was career-defining stuff.

This book concludes with Bowie's end-of-the-'70s post-punk kiss-off and apotheosis *Scary Monsters (And Super Creeps)* and includes a look at music performed for the 1982 TV dramatisation of Berthold Brecht's *Baal*.

Many Bowie fans see these as the golden years of Bowie's career, and it's true that every piece of music he wrote (from the dirty blues of his first single 'Liza Jane' to the edgy and weirdly uncompromising collaboration with composer/producer Georgio Moroder ('Putting Out Fire' for the 1982 horror flick *Cat People*) is revelatory. Within these pages, I hope to show why Bowie created the indelible music that he did.

Early Singles

Bowie released six singles between 1964 and 1966, in a mixture of styles ranging from R&B and mod to straight pop. All 12 songs, plus a number of outtakes and demos, were included on a compilation called *Early On*, from which this chapter derives. Inevitably, demos and outtakes just muddy the waters, though they give a feel of other avenues Bowie sought to explore at the time. However, if just the 12 singles and B-sides were included, it would still feel like an early album, showing how David's style changed rapidly even so early in his career as he sought his own sound – from the derivative but vital early songs to the later more Bowie-esque single 'I Dig Everything'.

Bowie reimagined and re-recorded many of these songs around the turn of the millennium as he became nostalgic for the old days, producing an album reflecting this called *Toy*. It was rejected by his record company, then EMI, but was posthumously released in 2022. The later songs are just as good or surpass these original versions. But the past has its own charms: mysterious and full of impossible-to-replicate innocence.

Liza Jane – Single by Davie Jones with The King Bees
'Liza Jane' b/w 'Louie, Louie, Go Home'
Personnel:
David Bowie: vocals, saxophone
George Underwood: guitar, harmonica, backing vocals
Roger Buck: lead guitar
Francis Howard: bass
Bob Allen: drums
Producer: Leslie Conn
Running time: 2:18/2:12
Studio: Decca, London
Release date: May 1964
Original UK label: Vocalion Pop, V.9221
Chart position: did not chart

'Liza Jane' (Leslie Conn)
David Bowie's first single has a fantastic saxophone-backed guitar riff. The song is credited to Les Conn but is well known to be based on an old blues song, and, of course, this serves notice to the world that Bowie was not simply interested in artifice: a criticism often levelled at him by people who see aspects of his work as *plastic* and lacking in authenticity. This is a raw and pounding R&B workout, very much in the vein of The Rolling Stones' early work. The twin saxes – alto and tenor – which drive the track along are extremely vibrant and give this first official tilt at the charts a real chance of success, though that was ultimately not to be. Still, the verve and attack with which Bowie approaches this simple song are not so far removed from later hits like 'John, I'm Only Dancing' and 'Rebel Rebel'.

'Louis, Louis Go Home' (Paul Revere/Mark Lindsay)
The second track on the *Early On* compilation and the B-side of 'Liza Jane'
is a contemporary track popularised in 1964 by American rockers Paul
Revere & the Raiders. It's essentially a tongue-in-cheek response to the
earlier well-known standard 'Louie, Louie': a hit for The Kingsmen in 1963.
Sung with exactly the same sort of insouciant attitude as so often sported
by singers of its well-known predecessor, 'Louis, Louis Go Home' is another
R&B workout, but this time with a few Beatles touches in the backing
vocals. In fact, one of the passages of backing vocals virtually carbon-
copies the Fab Four in their version of 'Money (That's What I Want)'. This
shows that Bowie and his King Bees were every bit as aware of the pop-
song format as they were of the blues boom's updating of old delta-blues
favourites.

Between the release of 'Liza Jane' and the next attempt at commercial
success, Bowie's backing band split up due to a lack of success, but this
precipitated a more calculated attempt by Bowie's then-manager Les Conn
to present a more representative vehicle for Bowie's expressive singing. This
time the band was called The Manish Boys: obviously a reference to the old
Muddy Waters blues standard, but curiously misspelt.

I Pity The Fool – Single by The Manish Boys
'I Pity The Fool' b/w **'Take My Tip'**
Personnel:
Backing band: The Manish Boys
David Bowie: vocals, saxophone
Johnny Flux, Jimmy Page: guitar
John Watson: bass
Bob Solly: organ
Paul Rodriguez: saxophone, trumpet
Woolf Byrne: tenor saxophone
Mick White: drums
Producer: Shel Talmy
Running time: 2:09/2:15
Studio: IBC, London
Release date: 15 March 1965
Original UK label: Parlophone R 5250
Chart position: did not chart

'I Pity The Fool' (Deadric Malone/Joe Medwick)
The song chosen to push the young singer's profile that bit higher was a
big hit for Bobby Bland in 1961. It includes a fantastic blues solo from a
young Jimmy Page, employed as a session guitarist, Bowie again displaying
a sort of insouciant cool in his vocal mannerisms, but this time with a song
allowing him to take a more laid-back approach. The presence of a wider

range of instrumentation gave the track more colour, but possibly, in this case, the saxophones were overdone and dominated the chorus too much.

'Take My Tip' (Bowie)
It is the B-side that really signals the start of the great man's idiosyncratic recorded odyssey. From the first bars, it's clear that there is a young songwriter with ambition and a lot of self-assurance. The song is a rather dreamy ballad, opens with a delicious organ motif, and includes some delightful imagery, referring to a woman as a 'tiger who possesses the sky'. It is a solicitous song, and the tip that the singer wants us to take is to avoid women who are too acquisitive or deceptive. This is advice that the singer might've wished he'd taken himself a couple of years later!

From this point on, Bowie was to write most of the songs he would record and began to show not only an acquaintance with the typically British songwriters who'd thus far been his main heroes (Lennon, McCartney, Davies, Townsend, etc.) but with the beat poets and Bob Dylan: the other obvious luminary of the 1960s. In fact, it's well known that Dylan and Bowie shared a hero: the incendiary and flamboyant black songwriter and singer Little Richard. In fact, Little Richard and Chuck Berry virtually single-handedly invented rock 'n' roll songwriting and effectively did for the black-American blues tradition what The Rolling Stones did for blues in England: updated it for the modern age.

Session Outtakes/Demos
'That's Where My Heart Is' (Bowie)
The rather forlorn solo demo has a flighty magnificence similar to 'Wild Is The Wind' and has a definite ambition to be greater than the sum of its parts. There are also intimations of Bowie's vocal inflections that would help make his songs so unique, especially on the line, 'I thought my day would come'. In the end, this is a proto-power ballad and certainly shows that most of the main elements of his songwriting style were already in place.

'I Want My Baby' (Bowie)
Again featuring only David's guitar and voice, this is another accomplished performance, much in the style of early Beatles hits. It charges along and reveals Bowie's magpie tendencies to be fully formed, as the chord changes and vocal style emulate the Liverpudlian hit makers with aplomb.

'Bars Of The County Jail' (Bowie)
This is a great little embryonic folk ballad and a precursor of such songs as 'Wild Eyed Boy From Freecloud' and 'God Knows I'm Good' from Bowie's second album. It's clear that his ability to give dramatic and poetic expression to a story has *always* been a sort of secret weapon in his songwriting armoury. Even on Tin Machine's albums in the late-'1980s and early-1990s he used this ability on songs such as 'Shopping For Girls' and 'Crack City'.

What he communicates in such songs is usually some sense of injustice, often relating to social inequality and shows a passing acquaintance with Dylan's early protest songs. In the case of 'Bars Of The County Jail', there's also a suggestion of pastiche, and Bowie's voice of woe as he intones the tale of a man falsely accused of murder has something of the mock seriousness of The Beatles' parodic cowboy song 'Rocky Raccoon'.

You've Got A Habit Of Leaving – Single by Davy Jones & The Lower Third
'You've Got A Habit Of Leaving' b/w 'Baby Loves That Way'
Personnel:
Backing band: The Lower Third
David Bowie: vocals, harmonica
Dennis Taylor: lead guitar, backing vocals
Graham Rivens: bass
Phil Lancaster: drums
Producer: Shel Talmy
Running time: 2:31/2:47
Studio: IBC, London
Release date: 20 August 1965
Original UK label: Parlophone, EMI 2925
Chart position: did not chart

'You've Got A Habit Of Leaving' (Bowie)
This is a powerful song with a very insistent bass riff during the chorus: a sound which bears comparison to Dylan's mid-1960s sound and The Who's power chords. Lush ringing chords usher in the song and allow the singer lots of room to rather dramatically excoriate an ex-girlfriend. Flourishes of harmonica give some colour to the song, but it's really the arrangement and fine musicianship that makes it work so well.

It would be surprising to me if, by this time, Bowie hadn't really begun to take on board Bob Dylan's coruscating cynicism and attacking lyrical style. The lyrics are very much in the style of 'Positively 4th Street' and show an awareness of Dylan's more sophisticated lyric approach. 'You've got a habit of deserting me' is a quite damning put-down, but when the chorus goes on to chide the song's victim with 'You could go on if you wanted to', it's clear that this is a situation the singer would like to change. But, as usual with Bowie, there is confusion about his emotional state: he's either 'so sad', 'so mad' or 'so glad'. The singer finds that he can't be happy unless he's with the girl, but she is deceptive, a recurring theme in these early songs.

'Baby Loves That Way' (Bowie)
This song has a fine, lolloping rhythm and an exuberant chorus sung by the full band. It is not clear what 'way' Baby loves, but there's no doubt

that the singer is prepared to accept any behaviour from his woman, including various types of cheating and abuse. In fact, he has encouraged her excesses: '...wants to play with other guys, so I let her'. The fact is that this song is a huge anthemic rock sing-along, remade with an edge of *ennui* as part of Bowie's aborted *Toy* project at the turn of the millennium. But it is curious that he has such an ambivalent attitude towards dishonesty and trickery in relationships.

Session Outtakes/Demos
'I'll Follow You' (Bowie)
The two full-band demos on the *Early On* collection are arrangements of songs that seem close to completion but maybe aren't quite as strong melodically or as fully realised as the released singles. The first of these is a sinister little ditty in the same mode as Lennon's 'I'll Get You' by The Beatles. It also shares its unsavoury theme with 'Every Breath You Take' by The Police: another song that appears to be sung from the point of view of a stalker. Bowie does seem to be fascinated with the politics of human relationships throughout this run of early singles.

'Glad I've Got Nobody' (The Lower Third)
The second of these demos, which includes other musicians, starts confidently with a strong chorus but then seems to rather lose its way. In fact, both of these Lower Third demos are quite mainstream offerings; Bowie is still trying to cook up his version of the Merseybeat sound or something along the lines of The Pretty Things or The Who. What the lyric again reveals is Bowie's obsessive musings on relationships – in this case, that he is fixated on one particular woman who he can't get out of his mind.

Can't Help Thinking About Me – Single by Davy Jones & The Lower Third
'Can't Help Thinking About Me' b/w 'And I Say To Myself'
Personnel:
Backing band: The Lower Third
David Bowie: vocals
Dennis Taylor: acoustic and lead guitar, backing vocals
Graham Rivens: bass, backing vocals
Tony Hatch: piano, backing vocals
Phil Lancaster: drums, backing vocals
Producer: Tony Hatch
Running time: 2:47/2:29
Studio: Marble Arch, London
Release date: 14 January 1966
Label: Pye 5815 (UK), Warner Bros. (US)
Chart position: did not chart

'Can't Help Thinking About Me' (Bowie)

Here, there is no doubt that this is the actual moment that Bowie, the songwriter we all know and love, makes his first appearance. Just the tone of world-weary disillusionment in the singer's voice, as he announces in the first line, 'I've brought dishonour', alerts us to the fact that this is a Bowie performance of complexity and depth. However, the song is ostensibly about a young man forced to leave home because of some unnamed misdemeanour; as with all the best Bowie songs, it has a huge undertow of unresolved conflict to keep the listener enthralled, and with metaphorical conundrums aplenty. Lines like 'Remember when we used to go to church on Sunday?' have that eerie resonance evincing a songwriter with ambition. Other lines like 'I wish I was a child again' and 'I wish I felt secure again' allow us an insight into the feelings of any young man leaving home for the first time. Without a doubt, there is some underlying need in Bowie's psyche to offer up only a partial storyline in the lyric. Like one of Monet's impressionist paintings, his songs can seem to merely touch on the nature of a situation, leaving much to the listener's imagination. The band sound is not more than perfunctory and is another reminder of why it wasn't a hit and why David kept changing bands.

It was enough to keep the critics hungry for more and have prospective fans reeling with that delicious feeling of alienation that David's songs seem to so effortlessly evoke. The single made it to number 34 in the *Melody Maker* music paper chart, although it did not appear in the official UK Singles Chart. 'Can't Help Thinking About Me' could fit quite easily on any future Bowie album (*Reality*, *Scary Monsters*, *Aladdin Sane*), and it would still sound like a typical Bowie song.

'And I Say To Myself' (Bowie)

The B-side is no mean feat either, beginning as it does with a ruminative bass run and a quizzical Bowie intoning, 'And I say to myself I've got it wrong, wrong, wrong/She's a playgirl!'. It's a great intro, and the song itself develops into a call-and-response affair with the band singing the title in counterpoint with each of Bowie's lines. At one point, he tells them, 'Say after me, I'm a fool', and they dutifully do. Again, the song's narrator is never sure of himself in relationships and is questioning his own self-worth and his girlfriend's trustworthiness, with a long series of self-doubting statements of his insecurity – not exactly Shakespearean, but a soliloquy nonetheless.

Do Anything You Say – Single by David Bowie
'Do Anything You Say' b/w 'Good Morning Girl'

Personnel:
Backing band: The Buzz
David Bowie: vocals
John Hutchinson: lead guitar, backing vocal

Derek Fearnley: bass, backing vocal
John Eager: drums, backing vocal
Derek Boyes: keyboards, backing vocal
Tony Hatch: piano
Producer: Tony Hatch
Running time: 2:32/2:14
Studio: Pye, London
Release date: 7 March 1966
Original UK label: Pye 7M.17079
Chart position: did not chart

'Do Anything You Say' (Bowie)
David was back to the mod template for this single, his second of 1966.
Again, as with the previous single, this was produced by sixties hitmaker
Tony Hatch, though this one is a little less individual than 'Can't Help
Thinking About Me' and is similar in style to Bowie's then-favourite bands,
The Easybeats and The Mojos. In the lyric, he's pleading with his girlfriend to
stick with him. He sees other couples go by 'hand in hand' and 'two by two'
and sings that he'll 'do anything' to keep his girl by his side. The single saw
him depart from previous band, The Lower Third, and take up a new group
of musicians tentatively named The Buzz. Essentially, though, this was a
retrograde step in terms of its musical and lyrical approach.

'Good Morning Girl' (Bowie)
This song is a little more playful and perky than the A-side of the single.
Bowie seems bemused by his current relationship, as he's so busy that he
hasn't got time to hang out with his girl; it's just 'Good morning' and then
'goodbye' – completely the opposite sentiment to the preceding song. There
is also superb scat-singing on this one, all mirrored by a cool guitar from
Hutch, David's friend with whom he later formed the folk duo (and trio)
Feathers.

I Dig Everything – Single by David Bowie
'I Dig Everything' b/w **'I'm Not Losing Sleep'**
Personnel:
Backing band: The Buzz
David Bowie: lead vocal
John Hutchinson: guitar
Derek Fearnley: bass
Derek Boyes: organ
John Eager: drums
Andy Kirk: trumpet
Pete Sweet: saxophone
Graham Livermore: trombone

Madeline Bell, Kiki Dee, Lesley Duncan: backing vocals:
Producer: Tony Hatch
Running time: 2:45/2:52
Studio: Pye, London
Release date: 19 August 1966
Original UK label: Pye records 7N.17157
Chart position: Did not chart

'I Dig Everything' (Bowie)
For this single, Bowie is again accepting the help of another trendy pop
producer – Tony Hatch – who was adept at producing a radio-friendly sound.
The song has a wonderfully louche and humorous lilt but is so generic and
of its time that it would fit on the soundtrack of the Austin Powers sixties skit
movies. This was definitely lyrically influenced by beat poetry and the whole
beatnik attitude which presaged the hippy era.

'I'm Not Losing Sleep' (Bowie)
Finally, we have this really swingin' little number that presages Bowie's
upcoming Anthony Newley period. David is telling us all about his woes and
his lost loves but assuring us that he's not losing sleep over past upsets. He
sounds like a chirpy cockney chap with no worries (or so he hopes). The
song was his last not to be attached to a larger project for a while, with all
the next singles forming part of the sessions for his first album, which would
follow in 1967.

Band Demos/Unreleased Songs
'That's A Promise' (Bowie)
Available on the recently released CD *Rarities 1966-1968*, this is another
great pop song, energetically delivered by David and possibly the same band
that played on his sixth single. It's another reminder that Bowie was already
capable of writing a hit if it were only presented in the right way. It's a song
with a driving rhythm and a catchy hook but seems to have never been
considered for release, and this demo version could be a rehearsal tape or
just a badly recorded demo.

David Bowie (The Deram Album) (1966)

Personnel:
David Bowie: vocals, backing vocals, guitar
Big Jim Sullivan: guitar, banjo, sitar
Derek Boyes: organ
Derek Fearnley: bass
John Eager: drums
Marion Constable: backing vocals
Producer: Mike Vernon
Running time: 37:07
Studio: Decca, London
Release date: 1 June 1966
Label: Deram DES 18003 (UK), 16003 (US)
Chart position: did not chart

Bowie's disillusionment with the psychedelic era and the 1960s mod sound led him to some strange places. Certainly, there were clear pathways from the world of pop to the world of light entertainment. Tommy Steele and, to some extent, Cliff Richard are perfect examples of this particular career path. They both had pop hits and purveyed an ersatz rock 'n' roll image initially but were certainly still very much middle-of-the-road entertainers in the showbiz style. But for Bowie, what were the temptations? What made him vacillate and produce not only standard rock ballads such as 'Silly Boy Blue' and 'London Boys', but also attempt to approximate the showbiz style of songwriting popular on what during the earlier part of the 20th century in Britain was known as the light program?

Surely, it was because at this juncture that Bowie may have been projecting for himself a more theatrical career. Was it just his because of his association with manager Kenneth Pitt, author of the earliest memoirs of an association with David, *The Pitt Report*? It would seem likely that this was not the only motivation for such a choice. It looks as if Bowie himself was drawn to the actor's life and projected himself naturally into this role. He has, in fact, referred to himself as 'the actor' professionally throughout his career and, of course, has acted in several films and theatrical productions. It, therefore, leaves us thankful that these early attempts to appropriate the cabaret performer's style of songwriting failed so spectacularly. That's not to say that these aren't fascinating and sometimes quite arresting performances, but they are songs that present a side of David Bowie that is diametrically opposed to the currently accepted picture of the cool iconic rock star.

In many ways, the antiquated sound of this album reflects Bowie's relationship with his then-manager Ken Pitt. Though Pitt was an older man, he did seem to nurture his protégé's love of both forms of music to which he was naturally drawn. The rock song was Bowie's known preference, at least from previous musical incarnations, and Pitt encouraged him to expand his interest in the melodramatic show tune format, at least as long as Bowie harboured ambitions as an actor or theatrical performer. Kenneth Pitt – who knew the theatrical and show world at least as well as the burgeoning rock one – appears to have given the younger man as much encouragement in his rock career as in the one to which he himself was more naturally predisposed, though he must've seen the showbiz world as a viable option for the versatile Bowie, as he got David a showcase gig for his middle-of-the-road pop persona The Bowie Showboat: basically a Sunday residency at the Marquee club in Soho, London. The young performer's career was certainly in the balance during the making of the Deram album, and he was as likely to plump for a Saturday night at the London Palladium as he was for an appearance at the Isle of Wight pop festival.

The odd thing is that the Deram album is very much a sidestep, and the songs display all the signs of incipient schizophrenia. Long before the obvious admission of a split personality (which Bowie makes overt with *Aladdin Sane*), all the evidence is already displayed on this first solo album. The songs fall into broadly two types: those which approximate the rock/folk milieu and have a recognisable place in 1960s pop culture, and those which hark back to the light program, reflecting a love of a very British sort of humour in the style of Peter Sellers, The Goon Show and music-hall tradition. The young singer simply wasn't sure which way to turn.

'Uncle Arthur' (Bowie)

This is one of the most successful of Bowie's songs in the music-hall humourist mode. It has a natty little nine-note riff played on organ and is driven along nicely by some good rhythm-section interplay. The story of 'Uncle Arthur' is the old chestnut of the boy who never grows up and becomes a middle-aged mummy's-boy. Though there is the sudden chance for Arthur to break out of his staid environment and cut mummy's apron strings, after a whirlwind romance and marriage, he finds his wife's cooking to be not up to his mother's standard. He ends up running home to her, returning to endless childhood a la *Steptoe And Son*, surrounded by his comic books and childhood accoutrements, never to escape.

'Sell Me A Coat' (Bowie)

This aspires to be another of Bowie's rather sumptuous ballads, and yet it also contains elements of the folk-song format, as if Bob Dylan had been filtered through the more middle-of-the-road interpretations of Irish tenor Val Doonican, popular in the UK at the time. Though the song has a folky feel and reflects David's love of acoustic music during this phase of his career, there is something a little too artificial about the track. It is a clever song, though, equating the need for the eponymous hoped-for coat with the singer's lost love. The song has a fine melody and envelops one in its warmth, rather like the titular coat, with 'the memory of a summer day'.

23

'Rubber Band' (Bowie)

This is the first song on Bowie's first solo album (1967), known affectionately as the Deram album. The song is an exercise in strangely morose humour and rather heavy-handed pathos. It is probably one of the least successful tracks on the album, and therefore, it's odd it was chosen as the first single. Yet stranger still is the fact that the B-side 'London Boys' is a much more successful song and is typically Bowie-esque in the modern sense, i.e. dripping with alienation and weird otherworldly undercurrents.

Where 'Rubber Band' fails is in its ability to convince the listener of any real sense of identification with the central character, who has lost his 'Sunday love' to one of the Rubber Band's members. I can't think of another Bowie song that fails to connect with the listener in this way. Bowie tries to invest the song with pathos, at various points making little comments aimed at the offending band member – such as 'I hope you break your baton!', but the humour falls flat. It is all very strange and leaves listeners scratching their heads in wonder.

'Love You Till Tuesday' (Bowie)

Another single, this is the first track to feature a Bowie vocal somewhat reminiscent of all-round entertainer Anthony Newley. He was an unusual influence on Bowie, and though he wrote and performed his own songs, he was really best known as a comedy actor, appearing in a number of films and a stage musical he wrote with Leslie Bricusse in 1961 called *Stop The World – I Want To Get Off*. Posters for the show depicted Newley as a mime in white face – an image that would become familiar to Bowie fans. Though some blame may be attached to Mr. Newley as the inspiration behind some of Bowie's attempts at comedy songs on this album, we must also be thankful to the actor and singer, as he gave rock music – via Bowie's obvious emulation of Newley's cockney vocal mannerisms – an English regional accent. In fact, Bowie was to employ versions of his *mockney* accent on a number of later tracks, most famously perhaps on the single 'Be My Wife' from the *Low* album (1977).

'There Is A Happy Land' (Bowie)

This harks back to childhood for its inspiration, dreamily describing children's games and daily activities as if they were entirely unrelated to the world of adults. The song aims for that sort of longing and poignancy that a yearning for the innocence of children evokes. Yet, even with its sumptuous melody and gentle orchestration, it does have a harder edge. Just a suggestion of adulthood encroaching on the land of the lost boys, perhaps.

'We Are The Hungry Men' (Bowie)

Heavy-handed humorous political satire was not really Bowie's thing. Here, he tries to deal with famine and overpopulation via the chirpy-cockney-chap routine he'd already achieved with 'The Laughing Gnome', the single that came out prior to the album (see outtakes/singles below). This is the song most reminiscent of a *Goon Show* script. Perhaps he should've covered their 'I'm Walking Backwards For Christmas' or 'Ying Tong Song'. The ideas in 'We Are The Hungry Men' were to be more seriously explored in the 1973 science-fiction film *Soylent Green*.

'When I Live My Dream' (Bowie)

One of Ken Pitt's favourite songs of David's, this is one in a line of songs drenched in pathos and with childhood's aura of the dreams and expectations of youth. A richly orchestral arrangement lifts this into the realms of Frank Sinatra or Tony Bennett, but with the recognition also that this is a younger artist with big expectations and ambitions. It has a fine melody and is one of a number of songs that were included in a showreel of David presenting songs from this era, and also performing his own mime piece, 'The Mask'.

'Little Bombardier' (Bowie)

This strange song has all the elements of a gentle music-hall pastiche – a casual, jokey vocal, a burlesque arrangement, a story that begins in a happy-go-lucky way (as did 'Uncle Arthur') about an old chap who still lives at home with his parents. However, the story develops into something quite different, and maybe it is meant to reflect some perceived prevalence of child abuse in the second half of the 20th Century. It is as if Bowie intended to write an old-fashioned song in the traditional music hall style but made sure there was a cautionary twist in the tale, modernising the narrative and warning listeners not to take everything at face value.

The song is deceptive. Even though it gives us a glimpse into the world of the past – as indeed does 'Rubber Band' and a number of the album's other songs – the implication is that not all is as it seems. No matter how much David wanted to signpost his love of Anthony Newley and his show-based repertoire, Bowie ended up with a foot still firmly placed in the rock camp. He has to qualify any suggestion of quaintness in the narrative with stark observations that the little bombardier may not be as innocent as he seems, or at least that he could be viewed in a darker way. This no doubt reflects Bowie's love of songs such as The Kinks' 'Dedicated Follower Of Fashion' and The Who's 'Pictures Of Lily': songs with a richer palette of descriptive imagery than was the norm for pop songs. With the string of singles released before the Deram album, Bowie had already shown familiarity with and love of those bands and other English rock acts.

'Silly Boy Blue' (Bowie)

Here, Bowie is signalling a newfound interest in Buddhism – a subject he took seriously enough to consider becoming a monk himself. This follows on from the song 'I Dig Everything' as it signposts his acquaintance with the beat writers, whose figurehead and most famous exponent, Jack Kerouac, was inspired by Zen Buddhist ideas. Kerouac's association with the Eastern mystical tradition may have piqued Bowie's interest and moved him to look into it further. 'Silly Boy Blue' is evidence that he'd done quite a bit of reading on the subject, as it is full of Buddhist concepts. The Tibetan capital Lhasa is mentioned in the first line. Lhasa is regarded as the holiest centre in Tibet, and the song also reveals a familiarity with other Buddhist ideas, such as the chela, a Monk's disciple. The line 'A chela likes to feel that his over self pays the bill' is an early example of a Bowie line using quite complex philosophical and religious terminology. The overself is similar to the psychological concept of the superego in Freudian theory – the lyric implies that someone starting out on the 'middle way' or 'noble eightfold path' (as Buddhism is known) relies on this higher self or guiding spirit to get things right, even if they themselves make mistakes: a concept not unlike grace in the Christian sense.

Buddhism played an important role in a lot of Bowie's early songwriting, even when not specifically referenced, as it informed other song ideas. Buddhist ideas were part of his philosophical grounding, and it is important to understand what Buddhist practice teaches – it is used to develop insight into the true nature of reality, essentially reminding us that this world that we perceive with our senses is actually an illusion. Reality is a construct of our higher self or over self, and ultimately of God or cosmic consciousness itself, which we exist within, usually completely unaware of its true nature.

'Come And Buy My Toys' (Bowie)
Central to Buddhist ideas is the concept of the impermanence of all phenomena. 'Come And Buy My Toys' takes on a deeper significance if seen from this perspective. It's essentially a litany of the toys that the narrator offers to his customers, sung with another accomplished melody and instrumental accompaniment, which could be termed soft rock. The song again borrows from the folk tradition, mirroring 'Sell Me A Coat'; the toys themselves represent ephemera from the material world – things we desire as children, and yet things that are, from the Buddhist perspective, like all possessions: transient.

'Join The Gang' (Bowie)
This song returns to the theme of Bowie's inability to fit into London's cultural scene. Because of his confusion over his career path, the problems he presents in such songs as this are hardly surprising, for not only does he harbour ambitions to be a rock star, but he also feels drawn – as we have seen – to music hall traditions, folk song and cabaret. The song has all the elements of rock, at one point even parodying the genre (at the end of the verse about a 'singer in the band'), and yet paradoxically, it's a protest song against the rock intelligentsia. Those who slavishly followed trends in the pop and rock world are here satirised and belittled by the same Bowie who himself was to become synonymous with such trends in a couple of years' time.

'She's Got Medals' (Bowie)

This has a certain rock pedigree, being based largely on a powerful bass-and-drums pattern, but also refers to the music-hall style. The song is a hoary old chestnut about a woman masquerading as a man – a theme beloved by folk musicians – but brings it up to date by placing the woman in the modern era. The protagonist is essentially a transvestite who becomes a soldier but eventually fakes his own death to return to life as a woman. Really, it's hard to square this song with Bowie's later championing of the gay cause, bisexuality and (by inference) lesbianism. The lyric possibly represents then-current Neanderthal attitudes to sexuality. No one hearing this little ditty would've predicted its writer's later dalliance with effeminacy, crossdressing, or his announcement of being gay.

'Maid Of Bond Street' (Bowie)

This shows a songwriter with great sensitivity and sharp observational skills. The subtle waltz-time pop parable describes a middle-class girl whose mundane life revolves around certain specific social signifiers with phrases like 'chauffeured cars', 'hailing cabs' and 'lunches with executives'. Bond Street itself – in West London – is famous for exclusive shops such as Gucci and Armani, perfume, art and antique emporiums. Bowie's non-materialist Buddhist sympathies notwithstanding, he was still fascinated by this lifestyle, no doubt wondering if one of these girls whose lives are found 'on the cutting room floor' would ever be interested in an ambitious young pop songwriter if we are to assume that it's from David's own point of view rather than an unnamed prospective suitor.

'Please Mr. Gravedigger' (Bowie)

As far as the original album is concerned, this is its *coup de grace* – a closing track that reveals Bowie's acting ambitions in triplicate. It's more a soliloquy, really, more spoken than sung, from the point of view of a murderer who at first seems only an innocent bystander watching the gravedigger work but who eventually reveals himself to be the killer of the latest burial. It's also plain that Bowie can't continue to hedge his bets in this way – either his music must be suitably rock-oriented in the modern idiom, or else he must give up this pursuit and concentrate on an acting career, with possible attendant responsibilities as an all-round cabaret entertainer. Also, the song is effectively the last gasp of his music-hall songwriting style. After this, he turned more obsessively towards a nascent pop persona.

Singles/B-sides/Outtakes
'The Laughing Gnome' (Bowie)

No self-respecting Bowie fan can be unaware of this great misstep in his career – an attempt at a jocular children's song of the type sung by kid-friendly performers like Danny Kaye or Anthony Newley. The sped-up voice of the cheeky answering gnome is very similar to The Chipmunks in the US and Pinky and Perky in the UK.

Bowie seemed determined to search for some way of attracting attention that still allowed him to make a living from music. He seemed to want to appeal to an audience that was essentially catered to by Beatles producer George Martin's early Parlophone records. Martin's remit pre-Beatles was to find and record quirky, humorous performers The Goons, a hit radio-comedy team in the UK during the post-war years. Had the Beatles not come along, it's possible Martin might've come across Bowie in this mode and thought him a perfect Parlophone performer. 'The Laughing Gnome', of course, belongs in this tradition and would've been a natural bedfellow to The Goons' hit 'Ying Tong Song' or the comedy songs of Bernard Cribbins, a UK actor whose hits like 'Right Said Fred' were constant radio staples in the sixties in the UK. Now seen as rather a millstone around Bowie's neck, this single is as good a silly children's song as anything by The Goons or Cribbins.

'Did You Ever Have A Dream' (Bowie)
The B-side of 'Love You Till Tuesday' is a mock-transcendental song with an out-of-the-body narrative similar to Talking Heads' later single 'And She Was', having ideas of the spiritual or astral travels of the soul. That it was sung in the chirpy cockney style of some here shouldn't surprise us, but it does seem odd that Bowie chose to make fun of one of the tenets of Buddhism that he no doubt took quite seriously at the time. From another angle, the many books of T. Lobsang Rampa (popular at the time) have a similar tone, and Bowie might've borrowed from this source.

'The London Boys' (Bowie)
The second track on the album's CD version, *The Deram Anthology,* perhaps allows us the greatest insight into why Bowie was so uncertain of which musical path to tread. The lyric describes a young man's arrival on the London scene and his desperate desire to fit in. The song even dramatises his first drug experience, and the queasy organ accompaniment – whilst emulating the sound of Dylan's *Blonde On Blonde* album – lends the song a bleary, late-night hallucinatory feel. The narrator is saying that though he's arrived on the capital's music scene, the hip London rock snobs won't let him into their clique and aren't responding positively to his pop persona. It is possible evidence of why the singer was forced to entertain other avenues of expression, maybe less fashionable and exclusive, which might give him a better chance of success.

'The Gospel According To Tony Day' (Bowie)
The B-side to 'The Laughing Gnome' follows on from the more serious 'The London Boys', continuing its theme of disillusionment with life in London

and the difficulty with friendship in an environment of distrust and ambition. Though the song is rather heavy-handed in its satirical sideswipes at his recently found city friends, it still shows that the groovy swingers the narrator has come across are really a drag and that he'd rather throw in his lot with the more reliable people from the established musical traditions that many of these songs hark back to.

'Let Me Sleep Beside You' (Bowie)
A single rejected by his then record company Deram, this is the first of two songs that are closest in type and character to what would later be considered classic Bowie – both sensual love songs recorded with producer Tony Visconti at the helm. They don't seem to belong to the 1967 phase of Bowie's songwriting at all but are really more in keeping with songs like 'The Prettiest Star' and 'Lady Grinning Soul' on *Aladdin Sane*. The lyric is full of romantic imagery, suggesting the young Bowie was becoming sure of himself in relationships with women by the time of its recording. No longer is he singing of 'white horses' and other clichéd imagery as in 'When I Live My Dream', but the imagery is now more knowing and suggestive of sexual intimacy: 'Lay your ragged doll with all the toys and paints and beads'.

'In The Heat Of The Morning' (Bowie)
This is a similar exercise in erotic metaphor, at least as suggestive as the 'Did You Ever Have A Dream'. The singer says, 'In the shadows I'll clip your wings'. It's all very languid and sensuous and no doubt worked very well as a live number at the time as David began his long quest for sexual adventure, which didn't end until the early-1990s. This is the aspect of his personality that would be a constant companion to his other image as the well-known alien chameleon. He saved particularly scornful laughter for anyone who brought up the chameleon label, though there was a compilation with this title in some European countries!

'Karma Man' (Bowie)
Recorded later than most of the *Deram Anthology* material, a number of Buddhist ideas make their appearance, not the least of which is the concept of karma itself. Familiar to many people these days through popular American comedy series like *My Name Is Earl*, karma is quite simply the cause-and-effect relationship between one's actions and the events of one's life. In other words, we find ourselves in a particular situation, in Buddhist terms, because of our actions either in this or in a former life. One of the most fundamental of Buddhist tenets is that of reincarnation – the transmigration of souls; the belief that after death, the soul at some point passes into the body of a newborn infant to live out another in a vast sequence of lives in pursuit of the ultimate goal of enlightenment. Another source for the song may be the science fiction book *The Illustrated Man*, a

1951 short story by Ray Bradbury (also a 1969 film), whose hero is a former member of a carnival. The lyrics in the song describe a 'Karma man tattooed on your side' who has 'fairytale skin, depicting scenes from human zoos' as Bowie reaches for a new level of poetic profundity with no trace of the humorous approach on the album.

'Ching-A-Ling'

This is a slight little children's song Bowie often performed at the folk club he helped run at the old Three Tuns pub in Beckenham. It was recorded with his first love Hermione Farthingale in the trio Feathers, with their friend Tony Hill. Versions exist with either Bowie or Hermione singing lead. There are videos of both versions on YouTube. The song was written in emulation of Marc Bolan's early acoustic Tyrannosaurus Rex style, as Bowie was impressed with his friend's ability to create instantly memorable singles that were earworms but had poetic, mysterious lyrics. The song was at one point considered for single release, though it didn't happen.

'Love You Till Tuesday' (Single Version) (Bowie)

This track, which appears on many CD versions of the album (including *The Deram Anthology*), is the song's second version. There is little to differentiate it from the album version, though the vocal is more quirky. Videos are available of Bowie performing this and other *Deram Anthology* songs along with a mime piece. He supported his friend Marc Bolan's Tyrannosaurus Rex as a mime artist. The films were all produced with help from manager Ken Pitt.

'Little Toy Soldier' (Bowie)

Throwing his lot in with another band – this time called The Riot Squad – David recorded this quirky and completely kinky song about a woman with what appears to be a sex toy – the toy soldier of the title – who is programmed to whip her and treat her badly. It's sung in a ribald, *Carry-On-*movie voice that says everything about the late-1960s and its so-called sexual 'liberation'. A miss.

'Silver Treetop School For Boys' (Bowie)

This Riot Squad song was a single by Glasgow band The Beatstalkers but only had David on backing vocals. It was not successful, though the quaint performance has some groovy 1960s charm about it.

'Over The Wall We Go' (Bowie)

Another comedy song to rival 'The Laughing Gnome', this hilarious demo contains the mock ludicrous and anti-authoritarian chorus line 'All coppers are 'nanas'. (Calling someone a 'nana' – short for banana – is English working-class slang for idiot). Sung from the point of view of a prisoner who dreams of escape, it contains a plethora of 1960s cultural touchstones like *Carry On* films, *The Goons* and *Dad's Army*. Oscar released the song as a single in 1967.

'Everything Is You' (Bowie)
With just a whiff of *Zorba The Greek*, this is a true anomaly in David's canon, with its relentless chant of 'bad-am-bad-am-bam'. It's not a folk song as such, but merely another attempt at a sing-along ditty that might break into the charts. It was recorded by The Beatstalkers (who recorded 'Silver Treetop School For Boys') but was used only as a B-side.

'Social Girl' (Bowie)
A nasty little ditty, this initially sounds like a ballad in the style of 'Maid Of Bond Street', but it has a beat-group romp, though it's only in a simple acoustic home demo form in the same stock as 'The Gospel According To Tony Day'. Lyrically, there is the suggestion that the girl in question has particularly loose morals. David appears intent on warning fellow blokes on the scene that this girl will go with anyone and break their hearts, perhaps leaving them with an unfortunate social disease. It's not the most inspirational of his early songs.

'When I'm Five' (Bowie)
A touching, simple evocation of a toddler's-eye-view of the world, eventually recorded with 'the Tony Visconti orchestra', which consisted of a number of their mutual musical friends, including Steve Peregrin Took from Tyrannosaurus Rex. It features David doing a superbly understated imitation of a four-year-old's innocence. It was written for a performance on John Peel's *Top Gear* radio show. It is unbearably cute. Visconti handles the string arrangement and other instrumentation with such subtlety. It's a fitting place to end the coverage of this strange and fascinating period of David's life. The track was finally given an official release on the album's 2009 CD version.

Space Oddity (aka David Bowie: Man Of Words, Man Of Music) (1969)

Personnel:
David Bowie: vocals, kalimba, guitar, keyboards, stylophone
Mick Wayne: lead guitar
Tim Renwick: guitar, flute, recorder
Herbie Flowers, John Lodge: bass
John Cambridge, Terry Cox: drums
Rick Wakeman: Mellotron, electric harpsichord
Tony Visconti: bass, recorder, flutes, woodwind
Benny Marshall: harmonica, backing vocals
Producer: Tony Visconti, Gus Dudgeon ('Space Oddity')
Running time: 45:13
Studio: Trident, London
Release date: 14 November 1969
Label: Phillips SBL 7912 (UK), Mercury SR 61246 (US)
Original chart position: did not chart
1972 reissue chart position: UK: 17, US: 16

David Bowie's first *real* album is a complete change, with only one track – the folky 'God Knows I'm Good' – sounding like it could've been on the debut. Instead, we have a true rock album, though with three more folky acoustic tracks – the above-mentioned and two love songs to his then muse Hermione Farthingale (could any name sound more romantic and fanciful?).

David's manager, Ken Pitt, had recommended New Yorker Tony Visconti as a producer, but the story goes that Visconti thought the single 'Space Oddity, was a novelty and, therefore, a sellout. This would've amused David, who expressed similar concerns about vendors at a free festival he helped set up for his Beckenham Arts Lab, which was similar to a folk club, in a room above the Three Tuns pub (now a Pizza Express), where anyone could get up and play (though popular artists *were* booked to play). This suggests they were both good hippies at the time. But it didn't deter David from forging ahead with Visconti as producer of the rest of the album, having already worked with him successfully on demos.

This album was originally released on the Mercury label in 1969 as *David Bowie: Man Of Words, Man Of Music* – a clunker of a title that owed more to his previous endeavours as a prototype humourist and crooner than to any desired career as a rocker. Culturally, this is essentially a 1960s album, with songs extolling the virtues of the hippy lifestyle, such as free festivals and the classless society. But Bowie had an eye firmly fixed on the future, and several songs in the set already prefigured the more nihilistic mindset of his glam rock trilogy of *Hunky Dory, The Rise And Fall Of Ziggy Stardust And*

The Spiders From Mars and *Aladdin Sane*. This new album would later be released as *Space Oddity* on RCA Victor (LSP-4813).

For all that, the album has a nice thematic and musical unity, proving to be a culmination of all Bowie's previous songwriting styles, and is a capably produced proto-prog rock masterpiece. What it reveals is that in the two years since the first album, Bowie's ears had opened to other influences, particularly in the British musical soundscape: King Crimson and The Moody Blues immediately spring to mind.

'Space Oddity' (Bowie)
This track had been given a serious makeover since the demo was recorded at the time of the Deram album sessions. The newly produced track became a big hit, eclipsing anything Bowie had previously released. A watershed moment in his life, the actual moon landing a week after the single's release helped to publicise the song, and a promo film was shown on TV: part of a video showcase produced by Ken Pitt.

The upgraded version of the song was the perfect tonic for the times, giving people a Beatles-esque soundtrack to the key event of the era. It captured everyone's imagination. No one could resist Paul Buckmaster's string arrangement, even though, in the end, the song had rather a dark twist in the tale. Major Tom (who would appear in 'Ashes To Ashes' in 1980) has no interest in returning to his home planet; in fact, he's happy out there in the great beyond, somewhat spaced-out. Whether Bowie intended to infer a drug trip or not, this was inevitably the interpretation of many, as it certainly fit the mood of the times.

'Unwashed And Somewhat Slightly Dazed' (Bowie)
This song signals Bowie's intent to forge ahead with his rock persona, leaving behind any semblance of the all-round entertainer. It has the feel of some of The Rolling Stones' then-recent stuff, with a lot of harmonica flourishes and duelling guitars in the R&B mode. It's also clearly influenced by Dylan lyrically, with lines like, 'My eye socket's empty, seeing nothing but pain', that could've come from any of the Hibbing bard's mid-1960s canon.

The song implies that the narrator is a parvenu, a lower-class pretender to the lifestyles of the rich and famous, one who can see that his upper-class girlfriend with her 'Braque' (an abstract Cubist painter) and her parquet floors is at once above him but intellectually below him. He is part of the 'strange unwashed and happily slightly dazed', quite possibly out of his head on something, but troubled by his insights into the high-culture morality of the well-heeled world to which he aspires.

The highly charged rock blast of this track also seems to be the first song on which Bowie presents his slick-tongued, sexually rampant persona, which was fully attested to at this time in the diaries of singer and sometime-lover Dana Gillespie.

33

'Letter To Hermione' (Bowie)

Bowie's love letter to his first true love, Hermione Farthingale, took the form of this melancholy reverb-drenched missive. The sounds are almost cavernous, with jangling acoustic guitars, the 12-string acoustic sound having been honed with his folk-club partner 'Hutch' (John Hutchinson), the two often playing as Bowie & Hutch and having had an earlier association with Feathers: a trio which featured Hermione's singing.

The song is charming and full of a resigned wistfulness, appealing to his muse to stay with him rather than move on to new pastures, as she was an actress and open to offers of work elsewhere. It was similar to the relationship between Paul McCartney and his actress girlfriend, Jane Asher, who had a similar conundrum that also didn't end well. In both cases, the actress did move on, and the musician was left to rue his luck.

'Cygnet Committee' (Bowie)

Beginning quietly with a lone thinker who seems to be pondering the meaning of life in the modern age, this is a multifaceted song with many movements and sections that reoccur and segue from one to the other, with a powerful progressive rock guitar sound in the heavier sections that grinds and churns, foreshadowing the sound of later songs from *Diamond Dogs* such as *Chant Of The Ever Circling Skeletal Family* and *Candidate*.

The song is almost an answer to Bob Dylan's epic *Desolation Row*. It aims to caricature the whole of society, describing the whole Western world as some mighty imperialist machine 'Plowing down man, woman/Listening to its command/But not hearing anymore'. This is the kind of curious, socially aware attack on the ills of the American dream (and British malaise) that many 1960s songwriters attempted, in one way or another, as they tried to put the world to rights. However, a more enlightened view of the song would be one that fits with Bowie's hippy idealism. This was the man who would later berate his comrades at the Beckenham Free Festival committee for being 'breadheads' when they took money for selling hamburgers and drinks to the crowd.

'Janine' (Bowie)

For me, this is the best song on the album, structured similarly to many of Bowie's later glam rock songs like *Velvet Goldmine* and *Holy Holy*. It has a superb melody and a straightforward structure, with the voice very quaint and distinctive. Lines like 'Your strange demand to collocate my mind/Scares me into gloom' give the song a very intellectual and serious tone. It bears comparison to other songs from this era such as 'Conversation Piece', which has a similar dense and novelistic use of language.

Janine is both someone Bowie wants to impress and at the same time keep at arm's length, which is another theme from this era – he may be coming into contact with women from wealthier backgrounds (like Hermione herself) whom he is attracted to but who are also intimidating intellectually.

'An Occasional Dream' (Bowie)

This is a gossamer-light folk love song that effortlessly recalls the quiet and sensuality of a new love affair, most likely his relationship with Hermione Farthingale. It is given a particularly magical touch with Tony Visconti's recorders and woodwind section, which seem to defy gravity, embellishing the tale with a special sort of grace and melancholy. David must've been enraptured by his friend's beautiful arrangement of this tune, and he sings it with his most precise and controlled voice, gently pronouncing each word. 'I recall how we lived on the corner of a bed'.

'Wild Eyed Boy From Freecloud' (Bowie)

This is a fantasy story song in the tradition of the folk epic, with a premise about an outcast who is really some sort of saviour – the 'wild-eyed boy' of the title, who obviously has powers that could help people, but who turns his powers against his fellow villagers when he is feared and rejected, destroying the Freecloud mountain. Bowie said of the song, 'It was about the disassociated, the ones who feel as though they're left outside'.

Many listeners would've misheard the supposed fantasy land of the title – Freecloud – as the hippy term 'freak out'. The song was beautifully scored and arranged by Tony Visconti, with a full orchestral layered onto the folky intro and the long rock section that concludes it. An earlier, simpler version was on the B-side of the original 'Space Oddity' single.

'God Knows I'm Good' (Bowie)

This was the closest David came to Dylan-esque social commentary in his early hippy period. He plays it ridiculously straight vocally, although in the delivery of the line 'tin of stewing steak into the paper bag at her side', there's just a touch of hysteria.

It is a masterful evocation of the plight of the poor and elderly and shows Bowie's heart is in the right place, also lampooning the simplistic notion of God that requires God to 'Look the other way' at the lady's need to steal food to survive and the similar hope that God won't look the other way when she is caught!

Superbly played on 12-string guitars, the song is essentially something that would've suited the first solo album alongside 'Sell Me A Coat'.

'Memory Of A Free Festival' (Bowie)

For the album climax, a motley crew of friends and musicians was invited into the studio – including Marc Bolan and his wife, June Child – to sing a long coda to this simple harmonium-and-vocal recital. With his quiet delivery, David takes us into his world in a way that allows the listener to feel that something magical is truly occurring at the free festival he describes. As part of his involvement in the Beckenham Arts Lab – a government-subsidised program that supported musicians and performers – Bowie was instrumental in organising the Beckenham Free Festival at Croydon Road recreation ground on Saturday 16 August 1969. He was there with Mary Finnegan – his girlfriend of the time – playing songs and greeting people. But in this song, there is also a fantasy world woven into the experience, maybe drug-related, as he sings, 'Someone passed some bliss among the crowd'.

When the conclusion arrives after a description of quite otherworldly events – 'We scanned the skies' ... 'and saw machines of every shape and size' ... 'and spoke to tall Venusians passing through' – there is a little hiatus, a sense of time slipping and then moving into another dimension as that mighty chorus bursts forth and carries us to the end of the album: 'The sun machine is coming down and we're going to have a party!'.

Outtakes/Demos
'The Prettiest Star' (Single Version) (Bowie)
Most Bowie fans will recognise this from the later version on *Aladdin Sane*, but this is the original single version with lead guitar tentatively played by Marc Bolan. This version is more spacey, with drifting keyboards underlying the gentle, effeminate vocal, which David intones sensitively. It is quite exquisite but belies the fact that Marc's wife June had a bust-up with David over the guitarist's role in the session, apparently claiming that Marc's playing was too good for Bowie's songs!

'London Bye Ta-Ta' (Bowie)
This outtake could've been a follow-up single to 'Space Oddity'. It's a lively pop song with lots of cute phrasing and backing vocals that connect the song to a gospel tradition, though the song is strangely secular and seems to belong in one of the Austin Powers movies, so fab and groovy is its feel. There are two versions – one is from earlier Visconti sessions, but both are similarly perky, and the stereo version may have Marc Bolan on guitar, as it's from the same session as 'The Prettiest Star'.

The song can be found on the *Sound And Vision* box and the 2022 2-CD edition of the album remastered by Tony Visconti, released as part of the *Conversation Piece* box set, which contained an enormous number of early demos for the album, and other discarded acoustic demos.

'Memory Of A Free Festival' (Single Version)
The concluding track was re-recorded and restructured into a glam rock single once Mick Ronson entered the fray, so the song was split into two parts and given the full Spiders shock treatment. But though it is an even better version – with Ronno scratching down the strings of his Les Paul with an almost punk-rock abandon – it still could not emulate the success of 'Space Oddity'. That was not to happen until much later with 'Starman': another space-themed single that garnered acclaim for its mimed performance on *Top Of The Pops* three years down the line.

The Man Who Sold The World (1970)

Personnel:
David Bowie: vocals, guitar, keyboards, harmonica
Mick Ronson: guitar
Tony Visconti: bass, piano, guitar
Ralph Mace: Moog synthesiser
Mick Woodmansey: drums
Producer: Tony Visconti
Running time: 40:29
Studios: Trident and Advision, London
Release date: 4 November 1970 (US), April 1971 (UK)
Label: Mercury 6338 041 (UK), Mercury SR-61325 (US)
Chart position: UK: 24, US: 105

Bowie grew tired very quickly of the persona he had so painstakingly created in the days of the Beckenham Arts Lab. He wasn't interested anymore in hippy idealism, and the new woman in his life, Angie was even less so. He wanted to follow in the footsteps of his newfound friends, such as Lee Black Childers – a bisexual fashion designer Angie introduced Bowie to, who was fond of flirting and dressing to shock and outrage. This was the beginning of what would come to be known as the glam rock era, and Bowie was inspired to recreate himself.

This led to the gig by Bowie's short-lived new band The Hype at The Roundhouse on 22 February 1970, famously attended by Marc Bolan, who at the show picked up a few ideas from his old friend. The Hype played their first gig with a lineup of Bowie, Ronson, John Cambridge on drums, and producer Tony Visconti on bass. David was Rainbowman, dressed in Lurex and pirate boots, with diaphanous scarves pinned to his clothes; Visconti was Hypeman in a silver superhero costume over a white leotard and a big, red-collared cape; Mick Ronson was Gangsterman in a gold lamé double-breasted suit and fedora, and Cambridge in a buccaneer's outfit was Pirateman. After the gig, they retired to the splendour of the main man's new palace of pretence and indulgence – Haddon Hall – where there were other friends who would soon be introduced to the new sartorial ideas of their leader.

Haddon Hall was a large red-brick, decaying Victorian mansion with castle-like turrets, converted to flats, at 42 Southend Road in the south-London suburb of Beckenham. The Hall had a small downstairs recording studio (that used to be a wine cellar) installed by Tony Visconti and David and used on occasion for rehearsal. David and Angie rented the ground-floor flat for £7 a week from the end of October 1969 to sometime in 1973. Ziggy Stardust came to life there, though the house was first to be the home of 'The Man Who Sold The World'. The flat consisted of four imposing rooms, a huge banqueting hall and an upper gallery, which Bowie liked to remind people led to nowhere. This was quite apt, as the next album was a rather nihilistic exercise, at least lyrically. The Spiders From Mars – Mick Ronson, Woody Woodmansey and Trevor Bolder – also lived in Haddon Hall for a short period, sleeping on the gallery above, while Bowie and Angie ran amok in their licentious underground lair. Trevor came too late to play on these sessions though, all the bass being played by Visconti. Haddon Hall no longer exists, having been demolished to make way for a new block of flats. In later years, Bowie often credited Haddon Hall, along with the upper room The Spiders used for rehearsals at the Thomas A. Becket Pub in Old Kent Road, Bermondsey, as the two main places where his iconic creation Ziggy Stardust was born.

In the dimly lit interior of the huge Victorian mansion, shadowy figures loomed. Mick Ronson – soon to be guitarist with The Spiders From Mars – came out of the bathroom looking debauched, blonde hair waving around his face. Bowie himself – sporting his new cockade of red sea-urchin hair – had not yet emerged from his basement lair. But in the living room, the queen of the scene – androgynous Angie – held court whilst sonic court jester Tony Visconti pulled the strings.

Bowie's entire intent on his first real rock album was surely to shock as much as to rock, and much of the subject matter is histrionic or quietly unsettling. Visconti has said that most of the lyric content was concocted largely on the spot, and so it acts as a cinematic snapshot of Bowie's state of mind.

The album was revived in 2014 when Tony Visconti and Woody Woodmansey built a group around them called Holy Holy and played the entire album live around the world. The vocalist was Heaven 17 singer Glen Gregory, and I saw them in Bexhill, UK. It was a memorable occasion.

'The Width Of A Circle' (Bowie)
The opening track was again mightily ambitious, in several distinct segments, similar to 'Cygnet Committee' on the previous album. Whether this was a reference to the mathematical concept of pi is not certain, but there is no doubt that the piece has delusions of grandeur, and pi – the eternal circle represented by a number thought to have no end beyond its decimal point – was a good symbol for the epic's portents of doom.

The opening gargantuan riff by Ronson has a circular feel. Musically sinuous, it winds its way through an aural labyrinth of crepuscular Hieronymus Bosch scenarios. Here we travel the many circles of purgatory, as in *Dante's Inferno,* for by this time, Bowie was becoming steeped in occult literature, demagogues like Nietzsche and Aleister Crowley being obvious contenders for inspiration here.

The free-flowing song opens with the line 'In the corner of a morning in the past', as if this were the beginning of a quest from some other era of history. From there on, the deranged persona David now took on – like a kind of minor Beelzebub from Milton's *Paradise Lost* – strutted his stuff, cocky and spouting verbiage, a completely 20th-century schizoid man, with Ronson's wild Hendrix-like lead guitar powering him on to greater flights of fancy.

During the opening section, Bowie, the erstwhile Buddhist novice, curses his master, complains about prayer, and finds that he's becoming a monster. But he knows he's 'ageing fast' and ignores a blackbird's advice to halt his slide into debauchery and go back to the mysticism of Persian poet Khalil Gibran. Then the song eases into a second section where the protagonist smells 'a burning pit of fear' and enters the flames of hell itself, declaring himself to be 'a spitting sentry, horned and tailed'. He's enjoying being a little Beelzebub. The song concludes with more heavy riffing from Ronno and a chorus of wails, timpani and massed guitars.

'All The Madmen' (Bowie)
The signature Bowie song from this period is a minor masterpiece of freakbeat – a kind of bad-trip in sound, including disembodied voices, 'The-Fool-On-The-Hill'-style recorders from Visconti, and a curious lurching rhythm embodying the zombie-like movements of the eponymous madmen, moving through a miasma of their own bewildered and deceptive perceptions of reality. The central thesis ('I'd rather stay here with all the madmen than perish with the sad men roaming free') is the recognisable hippy sentiment enshrined in the psychological theories of R.D. Laing, which claims that madness is in the eye of the beholder and that people deemed mad by society's standards may see the rat race of reality of those who are supposedly sane, as the *true* madness.

When it came to Bowie's current sense of self, there was a certain fear and loathing leaking from the flame-headed singer's head. This is understandable in many ways, as his half-brother Terry – incarcerated at the Kane Hill psychiatric asylum much of the time – was a frequent visitor to Haddon Hall. Bowie loved his brother very much and tried to welcome him to his new home, though Terry was something of a shell-shocked shadow of his former self. He was in the grip of schizophrenia, which caused him to hallucinate and disassociate from any social situation. When Terry arrived, the atmosphere was awkward. But Bowie found himself identifying with his brother's condition, finding a corollary in his own alienation from mainstream society.

But the gloom and decadence evinced by this track certainly seem to suggest foreboding about David's *own* mental state, and there's no doubt that the idea of 'a lad insane' would infuse his thinking throughout the self-serving 1970s. The Mellotron's giddy careening and the hare-brained drum fills drive the song to a deranged, gleeful conclusion. The US album cover actually depicted a gun-toting loner posed in front of a building strikingly reminiscent of the Kane Hill mental hospital.

'Black Country Rock' (Bowie)
We are now catapulted into a simple, almost bucolic scene where a peasant – maybe the travelling protagonist of the opening song – is resting on his

journey, a packhorse covered with his possessions. This is surely symbolic of the new individualist Bowie, happy in his own skin, finding that striking out for new horizons and beginning to see the shape of a future that is singular and arresting agrees with him.

The lyric suggests that the black rock of the title (if it's a real place) affords a wonderful view. The highest point in the actual black country (a nickname for the region surrounding industrial Birmingham in the UK) is Turners Hill, where dolerite – a stone containing black volcanic glass – is mined. The singer says it's 'crazy', but it's all he wants from life at the moment. He suggests we should bid him 'fond adieu' if we don't like it. In other words, if we don't like him or his companions and their lifestyles, he couldn't care less.

The short, simple and repetitive song owes something to those Marc Bolan was writing with T. Rex at the time, and Bowie's mimicking of Marc's voice in the final warbling cry is a delightful tribute to him.

'After All' (Bowie)

The last track on side one of the original album is as unsettling and as quintessentially English as anything in Bowie's canon. He doesn't seem to have quite lost the trippy sentimentality he sang with on his 1967 debut album, and there is something of 'The Little Bombardier' and 'There Is A Happy Land' about the 'Oh by jingo!' phrase.

With lines like 'Some people are marching together and some are alone', the odd lyric could be a version of the children's crusade – a medieval quest when young folk marched to take back the holy land; or even a song sung by the little people of myth and legend, who will put up with us adults only because 'We're just taller children, that's all'. The song transpires in a dreamlike netherworld where 'Man is an obstacle, sad as a clown', reminding us of those 'sad men' referenced in the second song, who roam in the rat race. The music is a whirl of wheezing keyboards and bass drum – not rock at all, but definitely a throwback to the 'Rubber Band' of Bowie's 1967 single.

'Running Gun Blues' (Bowie)

Side two begins a further descent into madness with this song which describes a deserting soldier – shell-shocked from his exploits in an unnamed war (likely the Vietnam War) – who declares hysterically, 'I'll smash them all/I'll kill them dead/I'll break the gooks'. A depiction of post-traumatic stress disorder to beat them all, the song takes no prisoners, its depraved, dehumanised soldier being a sorry wraith created by humanity's inhumanity. Synthesisers blast like battle horns, guitars drive on the battalion, drums depict their murderous march, and the bass bludgeons the listener as Bowie intones, 'I'll plug a few civilians'.

'Saviour Machine' (Bowie)

Another commentary on war, this time in a future scenario, the lyric reflecting David's interest in science fiction. He may have seen the movie

Billion Dollar Brain, where a giant computer is used as a tool of government control and suppression; an army general presents the 'brain' to the film's protagonist (played by Michael Caine). It dispenses orders to secret agents around the world, and this may have appealed to David as a likely vision of a dystopian future.

The music is a lot more controlled and inspired than on the other tracks, with a great characteristic riff from Ronson, giving the chord sequence greater drama and intensity. Moog synthesiser weaves between the chorus lines for a more futuristic effect, as the murderous machine informs us, 'I may kill you all'.

On his first album, he presented a humorous tale in a similar vein – 'We Are The Hungry Men' – likely inspired by the science-fiction film *Soylent Green,* which depicted a world reduced to recycling humans as food. Now, we are presented with a world-controlling automaton – a computerised godlike killing machine that takes over the world when it sees the fallibility of man. Though the song is portentous, leaden and a little unlovable, the playing certainly serves to bring the Saviour Machine to life: a juggernaut filled with borrowed human pathos, declaring, 'Your minds are too green/I despise all I've seen'. A prophecy of a grim AI takeover?

'She Shook Me Cold' (Bowie)

The central song on side two is the least successful here, being as it is a vehicle for extended free-form soloing by Mick Ronson, who goes all out for the throne so recently abdicated by Hendrix. The song is prophetic in some ways, as it prefigures many lascivious ditties Bowie would later perform as the lithe and androgynous Ziggy Stardust or Aladdin Sane. It is simply a song that extols the virtues of sex: 'I had no time to spare/I grabbed her golden hair/I threw her to the ground' moans the singer; 'My god, she shook me cold'. He's lost in the throes of his passion and thrashes about wildly with his woman. It is said there were orgies in the big, communal living space at Haddon Hall, a fact alluded to in the 2012 graphic novel *Haddon Hall: When David Invented Bowie* by Tunisian artist Nejib and in *Bowie: The Biography* by Wendy Leigh (2014).

'The Man Who Sold The World' (Bowie)

With the title track, we are back in a dreamlike reality similar to that of 'After All' and 'All The Madmen', where something nightmarish is going on. Though there is an old English saying that passing someone on the stairs is unlucky, this song's protagonist passes only *his future self* on the stairs, and this indicates something of the schizophrenia previously alluded to in Bowie's songs of this period.

'I thought you died alone, a long, long time ago', he miserably notes as the song presents its picture of *ennui* and poses the problem of a wasted life and a lonely death. Bowie was borrowing from 'Antigonish' – a 1910 poem by the American William Hughes Mearns, which begins 'Yesterday upon the stair,

I saw a man who wasn't there'. There are many ways to interpret this idea (the poem was based on a story of a haunting), but Bowie seems particularly taken with the idea that it's his own ghost or future self and that this is the person who 'sold the world'. Perhaps in real life Bowie saw himself relinquishing his chance at fame, giving up the commercial world of pop (his recent Buddhist leanings would support this) for a future where his younger self could be proud of him for his spiritual attainment. But a darker view – in keeping with the album's themes – would be that his future self somehow, in some kind of biblical sense, 'sold his soul to gain the world'. However, the confidence in the major-key chorus line, 'We never lost control', would suggest the former view: David and his future self agreeing.

The fuzzy chords, chorus rhythm and especially the scratchy percussion accompaniment are extremely haunting, and Nirvana gave the song a great interpretation on *MTV Unplugged* in November 1993, thus revitalising the song and bringing its weird charm to a new generation. Interviewed in the early 1990s on Dutch TV, Bowie commented, 'My state of mind when I was actually writing it was, I guess, as near to a mystical state that a 19-year-old can get into. I was studying Buddhism at the time'. He produced the cheeky sax-drenched version by 1960s pop star Lulu, which was a UK hit in 1974. That version's chorus is even more celebratory than the original.

'The Supermen' (Bowie)

The album's fantastic conclusion is the rather Teutonic tale of the Supermen. If you ever wanted to hear what an aria from Wagner's *Ring Cycle* might sound like as a rock song, here is a perfect example. With lyrics freely drawing on Nietzsche's idea of the Übermensch or Overman/Beyond-man from the novel *Thus Spoke Zarathustra* (1885) as much as from George Bernard Shaw's play *Man And Superman*, Bowie spins a yarn full of gloomy, high drama. The Supermen belong in England, or Britain anyway, as they are 'guardians of the loveless isle'. But they are immortal and belong to a time before recorded history, 'When mountain magic heavy hung', as in the Norse saga of Wagner's *The Ring Of The Nibelung*. But they also can be seen as inspired by the idea of homo superior referenced on Bowie's next album *Hunky Dory*, as 'the coming race': also the title of an 1871 Edward Bulwer-Lytton book where supermen control the mystical 'Vril energy', a term later espoused by proto-Nazis in Germany, who created the Vril Society.

And here is one of the less salubrious avenues of David Bowie's mind – he was well known to have been fascinated by the philosophy and history of the Nazis. He had books on the Third Reich, which were confiscated by East German guards on a journey across Europe in the late 1970s. He spoke of the power of Nazi propaganda; he loved the decadence of German culture at the time of the Weimar Republic and the Berlin of Christopher Isherwood's *Cabaret*. But at the root of it all was a fascination with mysteries and legends, the holy grail, mythology and a search for truth – like Shaw's play *Man And*

Superman referencing Nietzsche's idea of the superman, but as a higher, more-evolved spiritual being in keeping with David's original Buddhist ideals. It's just that with the beginnings of fame, a dalliance with drugs, free sex and the general overindulgences, he perhaps lost his way for a while.

'The Supermen' was often performed in a stripped-down four-piece rock incarnation live. But here, as the album's big finale, it was given the full treatment with those wailing, Wagnerian voices and timpani. The simpler band version appeared as an extra track on the album's 1990 CD issue. The live version can also be heard on bootlegs from the *Ziggy* era.

It is still a stirring track, and when Ronno's guitar is in the foreground, it gains another dimension, that man's graceful fingers always adding something new. It's the sound of a lost age, another world, a magical golden era.

Outtakes/Demos
'Holy Holy' (Single Version) (Bowie)
Released as a single at the time, with plodding backing from 1970s pop band Blue Mink, this is a sub-T. Rex grind with lyrics referencing sexuality and religion. It sunk without trace, though it returns to the rather demonic mood of the first track 'The Width Of A Circle'. Coming from sessions meant to produce a single after the album, it represents Bowie's first stab at a song that plays with ideas of gender roles and outrageous sexuality, though this is more apparent on the later Spiders version from the 1972 *Ziggy Stardust* sessions. This was soon reflected in a change to Bowie's sartorial demeanour, with a sudden need to cross-dress and express his more feminine side.

'Lightning Frightening' (Bowie)
This seems to be a section of jamming, faded in as if it had already been playing for some time, with possibly improvised lyrics. The music is almost relaxed – a slow, loping rhythm with lazy slide guitar all over it. There's no real sense of fright about the song, but it is interesting that the idea of lightning was already in Bowie's imagination here, as it would later become his visual *leitmotif*, burned into all our retinas on the cover of *Aladdin Sane*: possibly his single most arresting album cover ever. Of course, the subject of this fear associated with lightning is likely to be related to Bowie's preoccupation with his own mental health.

Hunky Dory (1971)

Personnel:
David Bowie: vocals, backing vocals, guitar, keyboards, saxophone
Mick Ronson: guitar, backing vocals, Mellotron
Trevor Bolder: bass
Woody Woodmansey: drums
Rick Wakeman: piano
Ken Scott: synthesiser
Producer: Ken Scott, David Bowie
Running time: 41:50
Studio: Trident, London
Release date: 17 December 1971
Label: RCA Victor INTS5064 (UK), RCA Victor LSP-4623 (US)
Chart position: UK: 3, US: 24

In 1971, Bowie began the phase of his most remarkable compositions. The continuing themes of otherworldliness and alienation are obvious. Inevitably – as we will see – these songs sometimes have arcane subject matter. He'd created an oddly distracted and effeminate persona and a new quavering voice that suggested melancholy and *ennui*. But *Hunky Dory* was still very much commercial pop music; even the songs with serious themes – like 'Life On Mars?' and 'Quicksand' – are extremely listenable. This is in part due to the careful production of Beatles sound engineer Ken Scott (who occupied the producer's chair for the next three pivotal Bowie albums) and the majestic piano of Yes keyboard guru Rick Wakeman. Tony Visconti had left the camp to concentrate on Marc Bolan and T. Rex.

The experimental phase of the proto-Spiders backing band The Hype had been given a new lease of life with the addition of Mick Ronson's tasteful string arrangements and his friend Trevor Bolder's inventive bass lines. It goes without saying that, along with Woody Woodmansey on the drums, this was a tight unit, capable of great versatility and verve. (All three were formerly in Hull bar band The Rats.) The Spiders From Mars sound was essentially birthed via the heavy-rock Hype performances on *The Man Who Sold The World*, evolving through *Hunky Dory*'s 'Queen Bitch' and on into the making of *The Rise And Fall Of Ziggy Stardust And The Spiders From Mars*. *Hunky Dory* wasn't a success on first release, only achieving number three after *Ziggy Stardust* was a smash in 1972. The highest US chart position for *Hunky Dory* only came after Bowie's death in 2016.

However, as the 2020 Bowie biopic *Stardust* implies, there is little need for The Spiders From Mars on the *Hunky Dory* songs, as they are still essentially (except for 'Queen Bitch') in the singer-songwriter mould. The movie (starring Sussex folkie Johnny Flynn) is a travelogue of Bowie's American publicity tour after the album's release in 1971, but the movie made little impact due to the owners of David's music refusing to let them use his songs.

He was presented as the floppy-hatted naïf who appears on the back cover of *Hunky Dory*, playing only covers of other people's songs, as Bowie did in his early career, though later in the film, he's miraculously seen transforming into the Ziggy persona, duly consecrated with his new flaming-red barnet.

It was really the lyrical impetus – the twin themes of alienation and fantasy – that delivered the spark that set Bowie's career alight. He finally found his own sound, and the melodies poured out of him as he found unusual chord changes on the piano and sang in a carefully nuanced phrasing. Nothing had sounded quite like this before. David's acute sense of late-1969s optimism, given extended vent in earlier songs like 'Memory Of A Free Festival' and 'Cygnet Committee', clashed wildly with his desperate need to present something exciting, new and relevant. His mind demanded a new forward-looking impetus of mental and sexual freedom, given free rein in his newer songs. Nobody could accuse Bowie of standing still or resting on his laurels.

'Changes' (Bowie)
This song starts with an intimate piano-led arrangement, its chords shifting restlessly like the sea or desert sands, coquettish saxophones underlying a stuttering Bowie vocal mirroring The Who's 'Why don't you all f-f-f fade away' in 'My Generation' with its drug-fuelled, youthful inability to communicate anything in a tongue-tied teenage stutter. The chorus has a gentle rising string section that leads into the measured descending bass line as if the singer is patiently getting to grips with whatever change throws at him.

Gentle though the song is, it's still a call to arms, like Bob Dylan's 'The Times They Are A-Changin''. But unlike Dylan, Bowie doesn't reference the Bible (no old-testament sensibility here) but rather Buddhism with the line 'streams of warm impermanence': the idea of impermanence being a central tenet in the understanding of Buddhist theology. However, Bowie takes great care to show that youth is the way forward, derided and 'spat upon', but always trying to 'change their world', and who, above all else, is 'immune to your consultations' (or as Dylan had put it: 'Your sons and your daughters are beyond your command').

With its bridge section, which begins with the line 'Strange fascination fascinating me', Changes also signposts Bowie's narcissistic self-obsession with all its fractured time-bound, culture-bound insecurity. He can't get beyond his own problems and mental fragility and knows that change is a double-edged sword: something that we struggle to understand but something we must always attempt to adapt to.

'Oh! You Pretty Things' (Bowie)
As a hit in December 1971 for Peter Noone of 1960s group Herman's Hermits, this was the first Bowie song to break into the UK charts since 'Space Oddity'

in 1969. With a strong piano backing from Rick Wakeman, this is the sound of David elucidating his recent tussles with literary giants like Nietzsche and Herman Hesse. He is singing about supermen again – 'homo superior' – yet making it sound like it's just the young and free who are aware of such things. And there are some very odd strangers appearing on his radar – perhaps glam pioneers: 'All the strangers came today'.

This is from the period when Bowie toyed with a gay persona, having stated in an interview at the time (possibly at the behest of manager Pitt) that he'd 'always been gay'. His comment was in no way true, as he was well known to be bisexual with a definite leaning towards heterosexuality. But he could be the figurehead of a movement for sexual liberation with songs like this, with its nailing-of-the-zeitgeist chorus of 'Oh you pretty things/Don't you know you're driving your mamas and papas insane?'.

'Eight Line Poem' (Bowie)
Arising from the prior track's fade-out, this song is a strange trip: a fantasy vision of America. Opening with a long guitar and piano intro, the scene is set for a description of the vast, wide-open spaces of the West. Giving in to his love of beat poetry, we get a Bowie version of Ginsberg or Kerouac, sung in a strained and effete voice, backing provided by Mick Ronson's country-and-western guitar-playing, over hesitant piano from Bowie himself.

'Life On Mars?' (Bowie)
This is a *tour de force*. Bowie was asked to write English lyrics to the French song 'Comme d'habitude', which was eventually more successfully translated by Paul Anka, resulting in Frank Sinatra's famous hit record 'My Way'. David's version having been rejected, he decided to come up with his own, showcasing just as much grandeur as Anka's version.

Rick Wakeman's piano accompaniment is so sumptuous, with a Mick Ronson string arrangement that fully lifts the song into the firmament. Shortly after the session, Bowie asked Rick to join his Spiders from Mars, but he'd said yes to being the keyboard player in prog rock band Yes just hours before. Wakeman has said that he found Bowie's chord sequence unconventional and inventive, giving the song unusual gravitas and an exotic feel.

Here, we are treated to Bowie's view of normal life as a reoccurring nightmare, where the song's heroine is forced to experience the same tedious movie over and over again – one in which earthly life is so grotesque that she is forced to ask if life might be better on some another planet, as life on Earth is so barbaric. It is ironic that this song, a big hit when eventually released as a single after the success of the Ziggy album, seems to imply that Bowie had an interest in the general theme of space/the cosmos, even though the planet Mars is simply used as representative of any other place that earth itself, where life is not so ugly.

'Kooks' (Bowie)
With its friendly barrelhouse piano and solo trumpet, this song sounds like it could've been played at a tea dance or as the soundtrack to an adaptation of P.G. Wodehouse, having a pre-war humour and charm about it. Certainly it is a fun song meant to be taken with a pinch of salt. But 'Kooks' is one of two odd songs that Bowie wrote around this time that seemed to be out of place amongst the album's other subject matter. Some – like 'Quicksand' and 'Life On Mars?' – deal with serious issues, but this one extols Bowie's newfound domestic bliss with wife Angie and new baby son Zowie (later renamed Joe). Though it's sung in the semi-hysteria of his new voice, he is really saying he's a happy man with a wife and child. Of course, there is the clear influence of Kinks songwriter Ray Davies in that eccentric, English whimsy, which can be so unassuming but humorous and quaint when correctly executed (like in The Kinks' 'Autumn Almanac' or 'Dedicated Follower Of Fashion').

The other song in a similar matey style was called 'Rupert The Riley' and included the unforgettable phrase 'Zoom beep beep' written in memory of David's first car. The 1971 outtake has never been released, but it often appears on YouTube. Of course, side-two opener 'Fill Your Heart' – though not written by Bowie – sounds even more like a 1930s jazz 78.

'Quicksand' (Bowie)
'I'm sinking in the quicksand of my thoughts', Bowie sings miserably. The acoustic guitars shimmer and shine, but it's the Ronson string arrangement that dignifies this rumination on mortality. Essentially, what causes Bowie's fear of his own thoughts is the Buddhist equation of 'thought equals ego' and 'monkey mind' – it never stops; it's always prying into everything, always feeding the ego. Buddhist meditation allows the adherent to still this constantly active mind, but at the expense of everything Western life is about.

The lyrics give in to a glut of references, stating the Buddhist word for a higher plane of reality – 'bardo' ('I'll tell you all about it on the next bardo') – and naming occultist Aleister Crowley's Golden Dawn: a society that promoted a magical view of the world, though mired in sex magic, which found Crowley nicknamed the great beast. More ominously, the song mentions 'Himmler's sacred realm', Himmler being a World War II Nazi who, though evil to his core, was interested in the occult and viewed the SS stormtroopers as knights, positing a secular Church of The Teutonic Order. Bowie always found the tales of the Nazis' search for the magical ancient Aryan artefacts fascinating. These rather sinister interests are further compounded by mentioning 'Churchill's lies', which – though there may have been many – are hardly what that great man is remembered for! In fact, Bowie is throwing everything at the wall just to see what sticks, claiming to be 'the twisted name on Garbo's eyes': perhaps alluding to the fact that the song is sung from the point of view of some kind of demagogue or a version of himself trying to adopt the mantle of the voice

47

of a generation, with everything *that* implies. In singing 'Don't believe in yourself/Don't deceive with belief', David was really saying that any attempt to understand the world through the physical senses, philosophy or especially pop culture, is doomed to failure – better to meditate, pray, and get in tune with the higher self.

Grunge band Dinosaur Jr. produced an almost perfect cover version as the B-side to their 1991 single 'The Wagon', though, inexplicably, they changed most of the lyrics to refer to the demise of their van 'the wagon' from the A-side.

'Fill Your Heart' (Rose, Williams)

On each of the next three albums – which includes *Ziggy Stardust* and *Aladdin Sane* – there was one cover version. A lot of Bowie's best albums contain remarkable adaptations of other people's songs. This one is by Biff Rose, someone Bowie discovered in America, an underground artist who exemplified the kind of outsider nature that came to be known as alternative or indie music. Bowie turned the rather dowdy original into gold. The music is jaunty and quaint, with horns that mirror the rhythmic 1930s-style rhythm. It's a simple song with references to children's literature (putting it on a par with 'Kooks': written for baby Zowie), like 'Happiness is everywhere/Dragons have been bled'. David finds the heart of this lovely little ditty and makes it shine, his singing voice a joy to behold: 'Love will clear the soul and make us free'. He sings the chorus like a funky gay preacher, and it is certainly the most spiritually uplifting of the songs on *Hunky Dory*.

'Andy Warhol' (Bowie)

Opening with groovy sci-fi synth sounds, this light satire on a theme of Andy Warhol has Bowie emulating Dylan's famous fluffed intro to his song 'Bob Dylan's 115th Dream'. In both, the singer breaks down laughing. We then enter into Bowie's ludicrous description of Warhol, the famous pop artist, making him sound more like the UK children's TV show character Andy Pandy: 'Andy walking, Andy tired/Andy take a little snooze'. Obviously indicating that Warhol's art is simple and somewhat basic, Bowie concludes with 'He think about paint and he think about glue/What a jolly boring thing to do'. Andy Warhol is said to have hated the song.

What's more interesting is the musical accompaniment, which wraps this little joke in a rich tapestry of acoustic guitar and backing vocals. Bowie sings his humorous lines with such gusto: 'Andy Warhol looks a scream'.

The song was also given to David's sometime-squeeze Dana Gillespie and appeared on her 1973 album *Weren't Born A Man*, produced by David, Dana and Mick Ronson. The video for the single version can be heard on YouTube. It's ridiculously po-faced and fully of its time, with the colour effects much-loved by TV producers of the time. It was not a hit, but later, Bowie productions of his songs for Lulu and Mott the Hoople *were*. Dana went on to be a doyen of the UK blues scene and has written an interesting memoir, also titled *Weren't Born A Man* (2021), featuring several stories about her relationship with David in his early career.

'Song For Bob Dylan' (Bowie)

This is a beautifully crafted tribute to Dylan, and uses turns of phrase like 'You're every nation's refugee', which have all the resonance of the man himself. There is also recognisable riffing from Ronson, which could easily be Robbie Robertson of The Band. The song comes on like 'Just Like Tom Thumbs Blues' and famously describes Dylan's voice as 'sand and glue'. But this is no criticism of his subject, as Bowie makes clear through his description of how Dylan 'Sat behind a million pairs of eyes and told them how they saw'.

What's curious is the chorus, which bears little connection to the verses, describing a 'painted lady from the brow of the superbrain'. Is this the whore of Babylon from the Bible's book of *Revelation*, who'll 'rip this world to pieces'? And at the end of the chorus, Bowie sings that however awful the painted lady is, 'A couple of songs from your old scrap book will send her home again'. What is odd is that it could easily be a description of the new queen bitch (see the next song), *Bowie himself*. Did Bowie see himself (maybe even subconsciously) not just as a bard who carried on the tradition of social commentary and artistic excellence that Dylan exemplified in the 1960s but also somehow as his antithesis, that artefact of the pop era: a non-authentic plastic pop star? It is a conundrum.

'Queen Bitch' (Bowie)

Lou Reed should've sued. This song – 'Some VU white light returned' as Bowie remarked on the album cover – is clearly indebted to Lou Reed and the Velvet Underground's template for trashy pop rock in the vein of 'Vicious' and 'I'm Waiting For The Man'. It's a fine testament to Bowie's skills as a mimic and his understanding of New York parlance that he pulls off a song that would've sounded great on one of Lou's solo albums. Bowie, of course, went on to produce probably Lou's best album *Transformer* a couple of years later. But Reed was always his own man and originated this style of song, with 'Walk On The Wild Side' being its exemplar.

The song describes a person up in a tower block, watching 'the cruisers' below, but goes on to reveal that the eponymous bitch is someone who has taken his place in a coterie of friends. 'It could have been me', he screeches, 'Why didn't I say?'. What he may have said, we can never know, but it doesn't matter because it's all academic. It's an exercise in bitchiness, backed by the kind of Ronson power-chord extravaganza that gave glam such a good name. Trevor and Woody truly lock into synch, too, making this the first truly Ziggy-esque anthem of the glitter age.

'The Bewley Brothers' (Bowie)

The concluding song starts with simple acoustic guitar and a few prosaic notes on acoustic piano through a Leslie speaker but ends in a weird netherworld of spaced-out, sped-up voices. It describes a variety of situations and scenes that depict surreal images of two people – the titular brothers – in churches and stranger locales, who are 'kings of oblivion', amongst other things. It's a song with so many unique lyric lines that it defies easy description.

In several interviews, Bowie was keen to connect this song to his brother Terry and to their friendship when Terry and he lived at their family home when Bowie was a teenager, learning from Terry's love of the beats and jazz – elements of the lyric certainly fit this description. But Bowie later commented that the song was a palimpsest (a document, often a medieval parchment, which has had the original words erased), immediately confusing an already perplexing song. So Bowie is alluding to this song being written over another older, different song. I believe he may be referring to the songs he so admired by T. Rex frontman Marc Bolan since the lyric is so redolent of the early Tyrannosaurus Rex that Bolan could've written it: his 1969 poetry book *The Warlock Of Love* being a key reference. Bowie admired the wordplay and insouciant tongue-twisting lyrics Marc pulled off particularly in songs like 'Catblack (The Wizards Hat)' ('a yellow orphan dancer rich in nature's costly gold wept for the jailor of time to bless her old') which was British DJ John Peel's favourite Bolan song, and 'Chariots Of Silk', the fanciful opening track to the album it was on, *Unicorn* (1969), with lines like 'a mad mage with a maid on his eyebrows hunted the realm for a god', which had a dense and diverting sound that producer Tony Visconti was so proud of.

The mood is immediately reminiscent of Tyrannosaurus Rex's early acoustic albums and could easily fit *Unicorn* or *A Beard Of Stars*. Two acoustic guitars predominate, and Bowie's background voices merge seamlessly with his lead, as did Steve Peregrin Took's with Bolan's on his earliest albums.

But it's the wordplay that connects the song most to Bolan's labyrinthine late-1960s lyrics: 'He's comedian, chameleon, Corinthian and caricature', Bowie sings. There is no doubt that the brothers of the title can be seen as Bolan and Bowie as much as David and Terry. But also, David may be conflating many friendships he's had – even his most recent with Tony Visconti, Calvin Lee Harris, Hutch, and even Freddie Burretti: a young fashionista whom Bowie met at gay nightclub The Sombrero, for this is essentially a song of male friendship.

The ending – an inexplicable throwback to 'The Laughing Gnome' – has a cacophony of sped-up voices meant to sound like 'the little people', gnomes, pixies and fairies, and also has its corollary in the early Tyrannosaurus Rex songbook. (Check out 'Strange Orchestras' on the first Tyrannosaurus Rex album *My People Were Fair And Had Sky In Their Hair... But Now They're Content To Wear Stars On Their Brows*.)

Another clear influence on this song is Pink Floyd founder Syd Barrett, who only lasted for one album as their songwriter but produced the whimsical little song 'The Gnome': one of many curios produced by the strange, lost poet of the psychedelic generation (found on Pink Floyd's first album *The Piper At The Gates Of Dawn*).

Outtakes/Demos
'Bombers' (Bowie)

'It was positively queer', sings David at the end of a 'Bombers' verse. If you ever wished to hear a camp version of the apocalypse based on Stanley Kubrick's movie *Dr. Strangelove Or: How I Learned To Stop Worrying And Love The Bomb* sung by an actor playing Peter Sellers' Bluebottle from *The Goon Show*, your wish has come true. Could this not have been sneaked onto *Hunky Dory* between 'Kooks' and 'Quicksand'? It's a marvellous piece, bonkers in the extreme but ludicrously catchy. The arrangement is very stop/start and miraculously precise; the Spiders are like a crack squad of session players. The final word's dwindling echo is priceless.

This track and others from the sessions can be found on the album's 1990 Rykodisc reissue, or you can get the 2020 4-CD box set *Divine Symmetry* – an anthology of songs from the *Hunky Dory* period, containing no less than five versions of this song. The 2023 vinyl LP issue inserts the track between 'Fill Your Heart' and 'Andy Warhol'.

The Rise And Fall Of Ziggy Stardust And The Spiders From Mars (1972)

Personnel:
David Bowie: vocals, backing vocals, guitar, keyboards, harmonica, saxophone
Mick Ronson: guitar, piano, backing vocals
Trevor Bolder: bass
Woody Woodmansey: drums
Rick Wakeman: harpsichord
Dana Gillespie: backing vocals
Producer: Ken Scott, David Bowie
Running time: 38:29
Studio: Trident, London
Release date: 16 June 1972
Label: RCA Victor SF 8287 (UK), RCA Victor LSP-4702 (US)
Chart position: UK: 5, US: 75

The alien renegade Ziggy Stardust now arrived from some distant star, intent on using rock music to pass on a message of hope and doom to the milling masses in the form of a concept album. The songs range from the balladic 'Five Years' to the wild proto-punk of 'Hang On To Yourself'. Much of the album presents a song cycle revolving around a world on the edge of apocalypse, but it's also a recognisable 1970s scenario of television, telephones and mass communication.

This album was also the last that Bowie would make as someone still trying to break through as a major artist. (It had been three long years since 'Space Oddity'). It contains his second breakthrough single 'Starman' – a perennial Bowie favourite and the album centrepiece, showcasing his otherworldliness, his love of the UFO subculture and the extraordinary in all its forms, including – but not limited to – the phrase 'hazy cosmic jive'.

The band on this album – forever after referred to as The Spiders – was now a well-drilled live unit, with many gigs played around the UK before the album's release, with Bowie in the guise of Ziggy Stardust. The first gig was at Borough Assembly Halls in Aylesbury, where in the market square, there stands a nice mural of the many Bowie incarnations called Earthly Messenger. Alien Messenger might've been a better title for the sculpture, dominated as it is by his Ziggy Stardust persona.

Though the *Ziggy Stardust* album doesn't refer to mental frailties or madness, as had songs on the previous two releases, after this album, there was a long, slow downward spiral in terms of Bowie's fears of the family psychosis and his dissociative psychological state, mirrored by a gradual rise in his perceived international stardom – a wild ride which really only came crashing down a decade or more later in the ruins of a massive, mouldering glass spider in a field outside Auckland, New Zealand.

The album – about an alien Messiah who comes to save the world with music – was a major success in England but was only a minor hit in the States at the shallow end of the Hot 100 (it achieved position 75 on the *Billboard* LPs & Tape chart).

'Five Years' (Bowie)

The opening chords of 'Five Years' are heralded by a quite special Woody Woodmansey drum pattern, and there's a sense of impending doom and lazy resignation. 'Pushing through the market square', Bowie intones as he begins to describe all the sights of the day on which it's been announced that the world will shortly end, its demise evidently to be in 1977. Though this proved to be an inaccurate prophecy, anyone who'd read the successful apocalyptic tome *The Late Great Planet Earth* by Hal Lindsey with Carole C. Carlson, might've thought otherwise. In actuality, all that changed in 1977 was the music scene as we formally knew it (especially in the UK) with the advent of punk and new wave.

In the song's crescendo, Bowie becomes hysterical (he 'felt like an actor', for sure), sounding seriously traumatised by what the song's protagonist is describing going on around him. In the lyric, there's the cop who kneels at the feet of a priest and a 'queer' who throws up at the sight of it. But more telling is the line about an unconcerned friend he sees 'in an ice cream parlour', still oblivious to the devastation ahead, causing our hero/narrator to experience paroxysms of fear and grief at the thought of breaking such news. It's a big ending, and the song comes crashing down with Ronson's string arrangement and howling, ethereal guitars soaring and souring the atmosphere as it all winds back down to the drums alone: melodrama of the highest order.

'Soul Love' (Bowie)

The drums enhance the album's first love song even more prettily on the album. 'Soul Love' again starts melodramatically, with the image of a tombstone, for this is love of many different kinds, reflecting grief, romance, sensuality and love-of-life all entwined. Bowie describes a series of scenarios in the verses where love is begun, tested or seen as sexually challenging, leading to gentle, reflective linking saxophone passages.

The backing vocals are as involved and intricate as any Joni Mitchell song – though unique and Bowie-esque in the extreme. Then those fiery block chords come in – Ronson's guitar full of fury with its wah-wah and sustained tone emphasising the end of every verse through to each chorus, tinged with Bowie's regret that merely *knowing* of love is not in itself actual loving. There is a sense of detachment lyrically that nicely contrasts with 'Five Years's emotionally charged catharsis.

Trevor's bass part underpins everything with restraint and poise. It's a truly killer track and surely could've been a hit if released as a single, though some of the lyrics might have been an issue for the BBC, as one of these loves being celebrated here is 'the church of man love'. It's one of several examples of Bowie playing up to his new gay-icon image. The idea of androgyny is endemic in his songs from this period and it adds excitement to much of the music.

'Moonage Daydream' (Bowie)

This song has been used in films – probably most famously the Marvel superhero movie *Guardians Of The Galaxy* when a spaceship flies into a massive space station through drifting space junk. The use of this specific song makes for a memorable sequence, with its kitsch lyrics about a 'space invader' who's also 'a rock and rolling bitch'. The lyric has a surreal aura – often nonsensical, really – but the music is extremely dynamic, with many power chords punctuated by Trevor and Woody's staccato bass and drums.

This signature Bowie and The Spiders song is also the title of the 2022 cinematic experience by Brent Morgan, which uses quotes from Bowie interviews for its narration, bringing to life his philosophy and feelings about his life and music. A performance of the song is included, with the melodramatic opening bars powerfully backed by clipped, overdriven guitar chords, as Bowie intones, 'I'm an alligator, I'm a momma/poppa comin' for you'. But he's not about to qualify that statement with any framing analysis, as the whole song is just a list of outrageous non-sequiturs, bringing to mind the line from Lewis Caroll's *Alice In Wonderland* about 'Believing six impossible things before breakfast'.

The song closes with a long, elegiac Ronson guitar solo that really is evocative, stratospherically atmospheric, and leads from the moon to the stars.

'Starman' (Bowie)

This song is Bowie's *leitmotif* – as seminal in its own way as Dylan's 'Blowin' In The Wind' or Bruce Springsteen's 'Born To Run' – and it cemented David's reputation in the pop world, giving him his first big hit since 'Space Oddity'. It also gave him a platform on UK television, where many fans in the UK found its performance on contemporary music show *Top Of The Pops* revelatory for its depiction of the androgynous Bowie throwing his arm over gold-clad guitarist Mick's shoulders in a suggestive manner. The song is celebratory, with a sing-along style similar to 'All The Young Dudes'.

The chorus melody is loosely based on the structure of the show tune 'Over The Rainbow', with that vocal octave leap. It mirrors a kind of quantum leap in the lyric, as the discovery of extraterrestrial life would surely be the biggest event in human history, the greatest change that could occur. This theme was to reoccur perennially in Bowie's oeuvre. His endless fascination with space started with 'Space Oddity', continuing with many other songs, from the reappearance of Major Tom in 'Ashes To Ashes', to the line 'Hello humans, can you hear me thinking?' in Tin Machine's 'Baby Universal', continuing with

'Hallo Spaceboy', 'Born On A UFO', and ending with some finality in the song 'Blackstar' with its sci-fi/ancient-aliens-related video.

When Bowie sings, 'He'd like to come and meet us/But he thinks he'd blow our minds', he reflects one of the most important protestations of the UFO community's apologies for the visiting ETs not landing on the White House lawn. In early Bowie biographies such as George Tremlett's *The David Bowie Story*, David is characterised as a UFO enthusiast, often staying out at night, sometimes on the roof, watching the sky, and occasionally claiming to have spotted spaceships.

'It Ain't Easy' (Ron Davies)

It's interesting to note that the title of American songwriter Ron Davies' second album was *U.F.O.* (1973). 'It Ain't Easy' was the opening track of his debut album *Silent Song Through The Land* (1970). Something about it must've really grabbed Bowie's attention, as he soon recorded this version during the *Hunky Dory* sessions, with Dana Gillespie on backing vocals. The track clearly didn't fit *that* album. One line of the song makes it perfect to follow 'Starman' on the album, with a line that always stood out for me: 'I jumped back down to the rooftops'.

David sings the song very softly, and the lyrics never seem clear. Essentially, the narrator is on a mountain at the beginning (like the 'wild-eyed boy from Freecloud') and is coming back down to Earth. Is this the 'Starman'? For David, did this represent the alien visitor arriving from above to guide us? He doesn't feel comfortable and is aware of 'strange things going around' down in the town. In verse two the song's protagonist hopes that 'patience and understanding' will help him deal with people, but in the last verse, it is a woman's love and attention that he craves. This is where the song becomes quite explicit (for the 1970s), and it may be what attracted Bowie to it in the first place, though he alters the lyric, referring to the woman in the song as a 'hoochie-coochie woman' who 'pulls him deep inside' instead of the more prosaic 'woman' of Davies' original lyric. 'Hoochie-coochie woman' is, of course, an inversion of the old Blues standard 'Hoochie Coochie Man': one of many titles awarded to blues singers, denoting their sexual prowess. This is where our visiting alien will find true solace it seems.

Though Ron Davies' original version is quite harsh, in the bluegrass/ country blues mode, Bowie's track is quite dreamy and a little subdued, with lovely keyboards by Rick Wakeman and haunting backing vocals by Bowie's occasional paramour Dana Gillespie. But it's Ronson's subtle and elegiac playing that really underlines the track's drama, as it ends side one of the original vinyl LP.

'Lady Stardust' (Bowie)

This song was sometimes presented onstage against a backdrop of Marc Bolan photographs. 'People stared at the make-up on his face' is a classic opening line, and one considered to be a tribute to David's friend Marc – lead guitarist on the original version of 'The Prettiest Star'.

This was a friendship that involved a good deal of friendly rivalry and eventually probably some jealousy on Marc's part when David moved on to be taken much more seriously than Bolan as an artist (though Marc's work certainly had its serious side – check out the 1974 album *Zinc Alloy And The Hidden Riders Of Tomorrow*). Bowie also name-checked T. Rex in 'Starman' and certainly recognised the enormous debt he owed Marc for his inspirational sound (also mimicking Marc's voice on 'Black Country Rock'). Marc must've loved these tributes, though they may have haunted him when he could only look on ruefully as his friend moved onto the *Old Grey Whistle Test* AOR territory that he himself craved.

But Bowie's tribute is a Janus-faced persona – Lady Stardust is seemingly an amalgam of many glam rockers. Elton John, Bryan Ferry, Brian Eno, and even Slade, Sweet and Gary Glitter are in there somewhere (not to mention female glam rocker Suzi Quatro. This is really a song that remembers the sadness in the portrayal of any artist who has taken on androgynous or ambiguous sexual characteristics in public. For me, it's American glam singer Jobriath I picture when I hear this song: a homosexual man who tried for stardom, failed, and suffered a sad, protracted demise.

'Star' (Bowie)

'Star' is certainly a socially conscious song that seems intent on reflecting the times Bowie was living in. It's a very English landscape: 'Johnny went to fight in Belfast/Rudi stayed home to starve'. It paints a pretty stark picture of the state of affairs in Old Albion, as the early 1970s was a time of some political tension, with the Irish internecine struggles ongoing, IRA bombings and the British Army dug-in on the Emerald Isle, streets strewn with rubbish as a result of industrial action by energy companies, and a general sense of malaise.

In England, this was a time when unemployment was rife. But with all the new kitchen gadgets and colour TVs, people were beginning to feel there was much about this brave new world of technology that was still amiss.

Throughout the song, David rails at the age he lives in and his homeland's state of decay, likely on behalf of disenfranchised teens and the dispossessed: 'Bevan tried to change the nation/Sonny wants to turn the world'. But the answer, of course, was to surrender to the wisdom of this new alien rock star, and Ziggy Stardust was ready to step into those huge, spangled platform boots and perform his wonderful miraculous cure on us all. Indeed, the song is somewhat schizophrenic musically, with the verses full of jerky, stuttering guitar and rock 'n' roll backing vocals. However, it ends with a long, suddenly bluesy coda full of tolling bells and slide-guitar passages, allowing us to wallow in David's daydream of stardom.

'Hang On To Yourself' (Bowie)

This is the album's most exciting song, shot through with fiery rhythms, gritty fuzz guitar, busy bass and driving drums, though it being a paean to hedonistic excess is not essential to any understanding of the album as a concept. That said, the sci-fi theme continues in the phrase 'praying to the light machine', whatever that may portend – certainly, it puts one in mind of the 1968 soft-porn sci-fi film *Barbarella*. Essentially, what we have here is a celebration of joyful and riotous immorality that only the age of glam could really have given us – the precursor to Frankie Goes To Hollywood's 'Relax', and a jolt of energy that's almost shocking in its in-your-face debauchery and degeneracy.

'Ziggy Stardust' (Bowie)

The title track has a hint of gloom from the start. It's a tale of tragedy. Those three chords with that little curlicue of lead and the descending notes at the end have been played by a million wanna-be Bowies in garages and rehearsal rooms the world over. The melody is instantly memorable and an insistent and turbulent B section leads to that three-chord pattern again and resignation to the eventual fate of the titular alien guitar god.

I always thought the song was about Hendrix ('He played it left hand'), but this didn't seem to apply to Ziggy's hair ('like some cat from Japan'). In interviews, however, Bowie unmistakably connected it to 1950s rock 'n' roll singer Vince Taylor (better-known in France than in his native England), who went mad and, rather like David himself, believed UFOs were going to land and change things on Earth forever. In the first Bowie biography by George Tremlett, the author remarks, 'I think it was the UFOs that took our conversation to another plane. Bowie tried to convince me he saw flying saucers every night.' Also, in *The Bowie Companion*, a collection of articles by various journalists, the writer Bruno Stein quotes Bowie, whom he met at an after-gig house party in 1975, as saying, 'I used to work for two guys who put out a UFO magazine in England, about six years ago. And I made sightings six or seven times a night.' In terms of inspiration for the character, Ziggy himself was inevitably an amalgam of Hendrix and Taylor and, either way, was certainly an extra-terrestrial sex god sent to save the seventies.

'Suffragette City' (Bowie)

This instantly brings to mind the dandies of the Victorian era, with a whiff of political intrigue and a city of the future filled with feminists. The song starts with heavy guitar chords and a nice groove accentuated by Moog synthesiser. The lyric is a coded dismissal of people who don't like confident women or who have entirely bought into feminism as a political idea but now can't relate to the standard 1970s sexual mindset. Bowie is fully committed to his 'suffragette city' (a personified sexual partner) but doesn't want Henry (to whom the lyric is addressed) bothering him with all the details of why his attitude toward feminist women is wrong. Bowie doesn't care, his girlfriend is 'out of sight, she's alright'.

The song has an exhilarating stop towards the end where Bowie howls 'Wham Bam Thank You Ma'am', a sing-along hook then leading to a sudden end. All of the album's tracks could have been singles, but this one even more so. In fact, it was the B-side of 'Starman', though it was also a 'turntable hit' that received heavy mainstream airplay.

'Rock 'N' Roll Suicide' (Bowie)

'When the kids had killed the man...' Bowie sings in the last verse of the title track, and here, he gives some sage advice to anyone in such a desperate, life-threatening situation. Like the resigned, lethargic, dramatic and doomy sound of 'Ziggy Stardust' itself, 'Rock 'N' Roll Suicide' has a languorous and positively downbeat feel. Though the song essentially offers emotional support and love ('Oh, no, love, you're not alone'), there is that title to deal with. Is this lost hope? An impossible mission? A hiding to nothing? Is this person doomed?

When the whole band joins in after the first half-whispered, half-sung lines, the track takes on a soul-review sound with bracing horns and *Wizard Of Oz*-type backing vocals, wailing in the hope of holding the subject of the song back from the brink, from the edge, from some sad end, from destruction.

In the opening line, time – personified – 'takes a cigarette and puts it in your mouth'. But by the next album, *Aladdin Sane*, time is no longer pulling any punches and is just another barrier to be overcome, another danger to life and limb.

Singles/Outtakes/B-sides
'John, I'm Only Dancing' (Bowie)

This non-album single ensured the continuing run of chart hits started with 'Starman'. It was issued in between the *Ziggy Stardust* and *Aladdin Sane* albums and was a clear intimation of Bowie's bisexuality. Two versions exist. This one has a whip-thin sound and a rush of adrenaline verses: 'Oh lordy, you know I need some loving'. It's lascivious and lush in equal measure, with Ronson's lead guitar parts meshing intrinsically with Trevor's bass lines.

The saxophone-smothered second version was included on the 1997 compilation *The Best Of David Bowie 1969/1974* and as a bonus track on the 30th-anniversary reissue of *Aladdin Sane*. It ends with a long, scratched screed of feedback from Ronson.

'Holy Holy' (Spiders Version) (Bowie)

Another track included on the 1991 Rykodisc reissue was this remake of the sadly turgid 1971 single released as one of the many flops in the wake of 'Space Oddity'. Heavy backwards reverb effects give the track a hallucinatory edge. Beautiful and strange, it's a night moth of weird intensity fluttering into the light.

Bowie sings, 'I feel a little bit evil/Feel a devil in me'. But though he sounds like he's in sexual ecstasy, he's desperate to find a way out: 'Holy holy, hold on to anyone/Hold onto anyone, but let go of me'. This later version – B-side of the 'Diamond Dogs' single, at the end of the glam-rock era – is a fantasia of shuddering sound effects, backward voices and incredibly searing guitar lines and is a fine *tour de force* for Bowie's new hysterical vocal style.

'Sweet Head' (Bowie)
This sweet treat should've at least been a B-side and has the most American colloquialisms ever crammed into one lyric. It's like David had been studying Springsteen's first album and borrowed a lot of terminology. However, the high-camp sex farce of 'Sweet Head' takes it one step further: 'Shazam and kapow!'. There had never been a pop song specifically about fellatio before. Everything is emphasised by another massive Ronson riff, and had the time been taken to beef up the guitar sound and finish the track properly; it could've been a classic. The lovely bridge brings in a touch of sadness and regret for such a song of wild sensuality, but it ends with more *joie de vivre* – 'move along, sir', Bowie laughingly says at the end of the track in the voice of a passing policeman – the sheer exuberance of youth.

'Around And Around' (Berry)
Bowie revisits his early rock 'n' roll influences with this rampant Chuck Berry cover. It could've easily belonged on the later covers album *Pin Ups* and shows off Ronno's riffing talent as per most of the album. The Rolling Stones also covered this one, and it's true that Bowie was at least as interested in their version as he was in the original. It is odd, though, that the song was seriously considered for the official album track list, as it did not fit in with the later claims that the album was, even loosely, conceptual.

Aladdin Sane (1973)

Personnel:
David Bowie: vocals, guitar, harmonica, saxophone, synth, Mellotron
Mick Ronson: guitar, piano, vocals
Trevor Bolder: bass
Mick 'Woody' Woodmansey: drums
Mike Garson: piano
Ken Fordham: saxophone
Brian 'Bux' Wilshaw: saxophone, flute
Juanita Franklin, Linda Lewis, Geoff MacCormack: backing vocals
Producer: David Bowie
Running time: 41:32
Studios: Trident, London; RCA, New York
Release date: 19 April 1973
Label: RCA Victor (UK) RS 1001, RCA Victore (US) LSP-4852
Chart position: UK: 1, US: 17

A lad insane? This was a brave album title, in some ways playing up to notions of mental illness now firmly in the past. The lightning bolt painted on Bowie's face on the iconic album cover may have been intended to suggest schizophrenia. But, in fact, in terms of its cultural significance as a symbol, it represents *sudden change* or a *fork in the road*. And if David had fears about his own sanity, in light of a number of family members (not the least of which was his half-brother Terry) who suffered from mental issues, he may well have been right. From this point on, there was definitely a move towards extreme emotions in his music, towards high melodrama, and the use of various substances to keep him engaged. In fact, in terms of his general health, this began a downward spiral that led to a world of drugs, groupies, insecurity, fear and exhaustion.

When Bowie got to America for his first major tour, his manager Tony Defries instructed him to 'act like a star'. Though Bowie was already a star in his homeland, America was the be-all-and-end-all for true global success. Looking like a truly alien figure in his outrageous outfits with a bright-red cockade of hair erupting from his now outrageously drug-enhanced head, Bowie was playing a role which had morphed from the alien rock god Ziggy Stardust into the madman and schizophrenic doyen of the arts, Aladdin Sane. He was ready for all comers, with an eye for the outrageous, the chic and the arcane.

'Watch That Man' (Bowie)
The opening song is a chaotic, revelatory explosion of erotic angst which alerts the listener to the nature of the life of the artist in the media maelstrom of this secular age, who makes his every move in the public eye.

The mix is murky, with the vocal quiet to preserve the idea that a party is going on. But it's probably a party only the elite are allowed into: Pop Stars

Only. The party has been thrown by Shakey: possibly a reference to Neil Young, probably the top of the tree for performers in the early 1970s with his hit albums *After The Goldrush* and *Harvest*. And the man to watch 'will eat you with a fork and spoon'. He's the main man, of course, the one everyone aspires to be.

With a heavy wailing battery of backing vocals, the track is as wild and wacky as an opening track could be, redolent of the Stones' recent *Exile On Main St.* album and full of scuzzy guitar with a superb wall of saxes. One day, there should be a remix with Bowie's majestic vocal more to the fore, as it really ought to be.

'Aladdin Sane (1913-1938-197?)' (Bowie)

The title track switches from the parties of music moguls to the more decadent and sedate parties of the pre-war cognoscenti. There's a woozy sense of drunken and louche sexuality, given life by Bowie's fantastic oozing saxophone and the laid-back, lazy melody of this reminder of a musical world before rock. Influenced by Bowie's reading of the 1930 Evelyn Waugh novel *Vile Bodies* (he listed the novel as one of his favourite books), it's an evocative piece, mainly characterised by the inventive piano of Mike Garson. Though the book is set in the time it was written (between the wars), Bowie's song saw fit to project another world war, with the bracketed years '1913-1938-197?' after the song title. Bowie has previous here of course, with apocalyptic visions like 'Five Years', 'Saviour Machine', and even 'We Are Hungry Men' from his debut in 1967. He's fully convinced that we will stumble into another war, just as the characters in *Vile Bodies* blithely continue their debauchery into the next war. With the Cold War still at its height, there was always a suggestion of 'wars and rumours of wars', as the New Testament's *Gospel Of Matthew* prophesied. We now lived in the shadow of nuclear Armageddon, and Bowie, in his coked-up, hyper-anxious state, was no less worried about the possibility than anyone else.

In a sense, this is the middle album of a trilogy with an apocalyptic theme, though here, the fear of war is nuanced and mainly induced by being immersed in the corrupt and wholly dissolute world of pop music; the discordant and heavily intrusive piano playing towards the end forcing us into an awareness of impending doom.

'Drive-In Saturday' (Bowie)

And then suddenly, we are in a vision of a post-apocalyptic planet, with a swinging 22nd-century version of doo-wop, powered by the type of descending chord sequence used in many teen ballads from the early rock 'n' roll era, full of 'dum-doo-wah' backing vocals. It's a masterpiece and was a hit single, with multiple cultural references (including Mick Jagger and 'Twig' the wonderkid' – Twiggy the model and cover star of Bowie's later *Pin Ups* album). That new-fangled device video is mentioned, along with surrealist technology ('Pour me out another phone') and, of course, an 'astronette', whatever that was in Bowie's typically fevered imagination. Later, of course, Astronettes became something even more desirable to him than this imagined presumed futuristic device: he named his backing singers after them and had a fling with one: Ava Cherry.

When the song reaches its climax, Bowie begins extemporising in a style similar to scat singing in jazz, which was to become *de rigueur* in some of his best 1970s songs, and it's my particular favourite in the nonsense-lyric stakes, with its many indecipherable lines sung over the chorus as it fades into futuristic oblivion.

'Panic In Detroit' (Bowie)

Here we're off on another post-apocalyptic movie-script ride into the emerging subculture of the gun nut. The song starts with the Bo Diddley beat and a backing of percussion with Woody's fantastic cavalcade of tom-toms. Later, a fluid Ronno lead line comes in, the bass rooted in the rhythm and subtly played. The vocal evinces that rather strained, slightly hysterical tone that David often employed, especially when he was in character for a pressurised lyric narrator.

There is mention of a 'national people's gang' as Bowie turns his head towards political chaos, riots and protest marches, then much on the news in footage of the civil rights social conflicts in America. Here, he envisages chaotic car chases and all-hell-let-loose in Detroit. What an amazing encapsulation of the smell of violence in the air that has so often engulfed the cities of the US.

'Cracked Actor' (Bowie)

Now, we are deep in the bowels of Hollywood, lost in a labyrinth of loneliness and pain. An aged actor spins his yarn about 'liaisons dangereuses' and his lust for younger women. The track has the most dirty, ominous chugging riff imaginable, which Ronson perpetrates with evil glee. The Bowie vocal is again histrionic, signifying his donning of another theatrical mask, which was accentuated on stage with a prop not used in any other situation I know of other than the famous *Hamlet* soliloquy. Hamlet's lines, spoken to the skull of his friend, are sad and regretful, but here there is only a disreputable old ham with his loathing of himself and everyone around him: 'Sold you illusion for a bagful of cheques/You made a bad connection 'cause I just want your sex'.

'Time' (Bowie)

When the mind is racing and the adrenalin of the performer is high, there is a curious effect of time either slowing down dreadfully or flying by like sand running through an hourglass. This song is meant to tune in to the artist's state of mind as they approach another performance, in thrall to every whim of the audience, the record company, the band and hangers-on. Time is the enemy, who 'flexes like a whore'.

The track begins with a 1920s-style stride piano, like the title track with its allusions to life between the wars. It is self-conscious, putting us in the performer's boots, treading the boards.

The song has a resigned, world-weary tone, as if there is an enormous weight upon the singer's shoulders, and of course, with fame, that is always the case. The guitars chime as Ronno runs through a series of countermelodies as ever, his arrangement skills easily as important as his playing, giving Bowie's album centrepiece its necessary pathos and depth. The bass is the track's core, providing a delicious underpinning, and the drums are carefully played with many filigree touches that serve to emphasise key lyric lines. 'We should be on by now', Bowie sings, the artist waiting for his moment in the limelight – or, as some people think, waiting for the drugs to kick in.

It goes without saying that Bowie employs his hysterical voice in several sections, not least on the line that would've shocked at the time, 'falls wanking to the floor' – an insult aimed at time to belittle it perhaps. Though, as we all know, time always wins.

'The Prettiest Star' (Bowie)
This is an update of the original single from 1970. All of Bolan's guitar parts were copied exactly, but with Mick Ronson's fuller, fatter guitar tone and doo-wop background vocals. The vocal has a certain fey knowingness (which on the original single was strangely innocent) as if he was updating it for the more world-weary character of Aladdin Sane.

The song was dedicated to Bowie's wife Angie but is a simply beautiful love song.

'Let's Spend The Night Together' (Jagger, Richards)
'All The Young Dudes' might've fit on the album perfectly here if Bowie had completed his own version. Mott the Hoople had agreed to take it and turned it into a massive UK hit. Bowie gave it to singer Ian Hunter and his band when they were at the end of their tether after several failed attempts to write a hit, though their albums were memorable and their wild live concerts legendary. Bowie was a fan. 'All The Young Dudes' saved their career.

But instead of that possibility, we get a ludicrously overwrought and sensationalised cover of the old Rolling Stones song. Other than the power chords and otherworldly sound effects, it's not much different to their original, although anything Bowie sings has a touch of ineffable magic, and many glam-rock fans would not have batted an eyelid, believing it to be another Bowie original with its heavy-breathing faux-sexual theatrics. His big lyric addition is the spoken section: 'They said that we were too young/And our kind of love was no fun/But do it/Let's Make Love'. This is followed by a bump-and-grind guitar fretboard slur from Ronno's armoury of guitar effects, meant to denote sexual activity.

'The Jean Genie' (Bowie)

A hit single with a great arrangement and interlacing Ronson guitar parts, the song title alludes to French kleptomaniac Jean Genet – gay icon and social outcast – whose erotic writings were occasionally obscene and who was a leading figure in French avant-garde theatre. Bowie was no doubt drawn to the writer as a social and sexual outsider, later commenting that the title was 'a clumsy pun upon Jean Genet'. A later video of the song used clips from Genet's short film *Un Chant d'Amour*.

The lyric describes a character who sounds like a refugee from a 1950s sci-fi film, 'who can't drive his module and bites on the neon'. However, crucially for the 1970s, he also 'loves to be loved'. Bowie wrote the lyric to impress Cyrinda Foxe – the woman in the Mick Rock-directed video for the song – at her apartment in New York.

The guitar riff, an old chestnut from many blues songs, was also mined by glam-rock band The Sweet for their single 'Blockbuster', which was out at the same time as 'The Jean Genie' (and was equally bonkers lyrically but was inspired by the blockbuster bombs used during the Second World War – their version included sirens). Bowie said that though the title is a pun on the name Genet, a more tangible model for the song's character was David's friend Iggy Pop, or Ziggy as a New York 'street rat'.

'Lady Grinning Soul' (Bowie)

For the closing number, David chose to bear his soul. He did not want to sign off with another strange diatribe (as he had on *Hunky Dory* with 'The Bewlay Brothers') or with gloomy superhero stuff like 'Supermen' (which ended *The Man Who Sold The World*. This time, he wanted something soulful and something that showed his inner man to some degree. What it describes is the title's object of desire. But what it reveals about Bowie is that he was a consummate observer – a man who had an eye for detail in his relationships with women and, in the end, was always at the mercy of their desires. That his lady has a 'grinning soul' is more likely a reference to her preference for soul music as much as it might denote her happily uninhibited inner soulfulness. Was it a portrait of a black lover? An early insight into his appreciation of their particular qualities both physical and spiritual? The music is languorous with flamboyant Flamenco eruptions but is also typified by that lovely, trilling, fragile piano iridescence that Mike Garson excelled in. It's a cool, quivering edging of lace on the track's elegant curve of sculpted sonic beauty.

Outtakes/B-sides
'All The Young Dudes' (Bowie)

Here, Bowie captured the essence of the moody teen experience of life. The original lyric with its downtrodden working-class protagonist 'stealing clothes from Marks & Sparks' is so hilariously English. A recording from the *Aladdin*

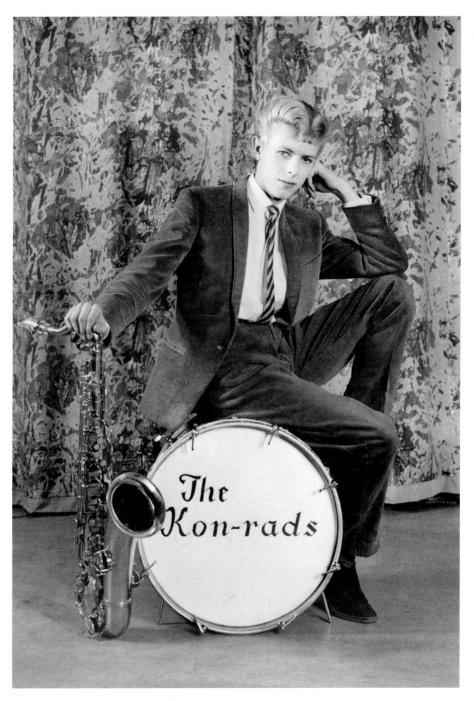

Above: David Bowie with his first love, the saxophone, whilst a member of The Konrads (1963). (*Roy Ainsworth/V&A/PA*)

Left: Chirpy Cockney Dave circa 1967 on the cover of his first album. (*Deram*)

Right: Bubbleheaded David with his Bob Dylan 'do' on the cover of his second solo album, later referred to as *Space Oddity* (1969). (*Mercury*)

Left: Alien Bowie on the back of his *Space Oddity* album cover. Painted by friend George Underwood, it depicts a cryptic scene based on ideas sketched by Bowie himself. (*Mercury*)

Right: David in his designer Mr Fish dress on the cover of his third album *The Man Who Sold The World* (1969) – a very strange album showcasing songs about schizophrenia, war and mythology. (*Mercury*)

Left: The US cover of *The Man Who Sold The World* shows an image of The Cane Hill Psychiatric Hospital, where his half-brother Terry was a patient. (*Mercury*)

Right: *Hunky Dory* was where Bowie hit a vein of pure songwriting gold. Bowie's feminine makeover for the cover was supposedly in homage to Marlene Dietrich. (*RCA*)

Above: Bowie's first glam rock band The Hype only played one gig at the Roundhouse in London in 1970. The band included Bowie, guitarist Mick Ronson, bassist and record producer Tony Visconti and drummer John Cambridge. (*Ray Stevenson*)

Below: It was when David formed his band The Spiders From Mars in 1971, with guitarist Mick Ronson, bassist Trevor Bolder and drummer Woody Woodmansy – all Yorkshiremen like David's dad – that he hit the big time. (*Alamy*)

Right: Mick Ronson, Bowie's right-hand man in The Spiders From Mars, played the searing and virtuosic lead guitar and wrote string arrangements for many of the songs. (*Foster/Retna*)

Below: Bowie, Ronson and Woodmansy.

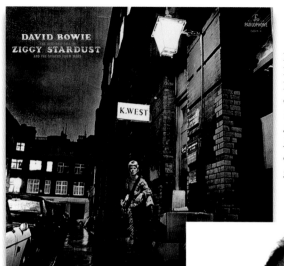

Left: David poses in Heddon Street, central London, for the cover of his first big hit album *The Rise & Fall Of Ziggy Stardust & The Spiders From Mars* – looking every bit the alien rock god. (*RCA*)

Right: The cover of *Aladdin Sane* (1973) consolidated the success of *Ziggy Stardust* and is surely a candidate for the most iconic album cover of all time. (*RCA*)

Left: For the front cover of *Pin Ups*, released after the break-up of The Spiders, Bowie posed with the model 'Twiggy', who is also mentioned in the lyrics to his song 'Drive-In Saturday'. (*RCA*)

Above: *Diamond Dogs* was perhaps Bowie's early masterpiece. Guy Peellaert's artwork, depicting the artist as a dog, was controversial due to the inclusion of the canine Bowie's genitals. (*RCA*)

Above: The image on the inside of the gatefold sleeve for *Diamond Dogs* included David's gruesome poem 'Future Legend'. (*RCA*)

Above: Between *Pin Ups* and *Diamond Dogs*, Bowie performed on US TV show *The 1980 Floor Show* accompanied by vocal trio The Astronettes, as well as other artists such as Marianne Faithful, who dressed for the occasion as a 'naughty' nun.

Below: Bowie's sketches were used to design the 'Hunger City' stage set during the *Diamond Dogs* tour, the album's songs originally being based on the George Orwell dystopian novel *1984*.

Above: David made many friends in the States; amongst the most famous was John Lennon, who co-wrote 'Fame' along with Bowie and new guitar maestro Carlos Alomar. (*Ron Galella/WireImage*)

Below: Bowie's drug-fuelled lifestyle was growing in intensity in Los Angeles in the mid-seventies, leading to a number of disturbing public appearances where he seemed disoriented. (*Bob Gruen*)

Left: The cover of David's soul pastiche album *Young Americans* was released in 1974 and took his profile to new heights in the States, where the single 'Fame' was his biggest hit yet. (*RCA*)

Right: The dense and mannered *Station To Station* is an album that Bowie, as he repeatedly remarked, could hardly remember recording, but many of his fans consider it another masterpiece. (*RCA*)

Left: Bowie as Thomas Jerome Newton, the alien in *The Man Who Fell To Earth*, on the cover of *Low* (1976). (*RCA*)

Right: The middle album in the so-called Berlin trilogy, *"Heroes"* contains some of David's most detached and deranged music, as well as the hit title track. (*RCA*)

Left: The gatefold sleeve for *Lodger* (1979) shows Bowie in a strange, 'squashed' pose as if he'd fallen from a great height. The image was inspired by the paintings of Egon Schiele. (*RCA*)

Right: Bowie's first album of the 1980s – a magisterial production by David and Tony Visconti – contains a number of hits, including 'Ashes To Ashes', which refers back to the character of Major Tom. (*RCA*)

Left: After the *Station To Station* album, Bowie decamped to New Mexico to film *The Man Who Fell To Earth*, working with director Nic Roeg, who believed he was a perfect fit for the role of an alien. (*Allstar/British Lion/ Studiocanal*)

Right: Bowie took off to Berlin in 1977, trying to clean up his lifestyle with his close friend and musical hero Iggy Pop. (*Rex/Shutterstock*)

Left: In Hansa Ton Studios, Berlin, where he kept a 'low profile', Bowie worked with Brian Eno and, later, Robert Fripp to produce music unlike anything he'd ever attempted before. (*Getty Images*)

Right: Robert Fripp's guitar playing was called upon to grace *"Heroes"* and *Scary Monsters And Super Creeps.*

Left: Maverick genius Tony Visconti not only helped Bowie at the beginning of his career but also helped produce the Berlin trilogy of albums that is the centrepiece of his oeuvre. (*Tony Visconti*)

Right: Brian Eno's input on Bowie's Berlin period albums cannot be overestimated. (*Erica Echenberg/Redferns*)

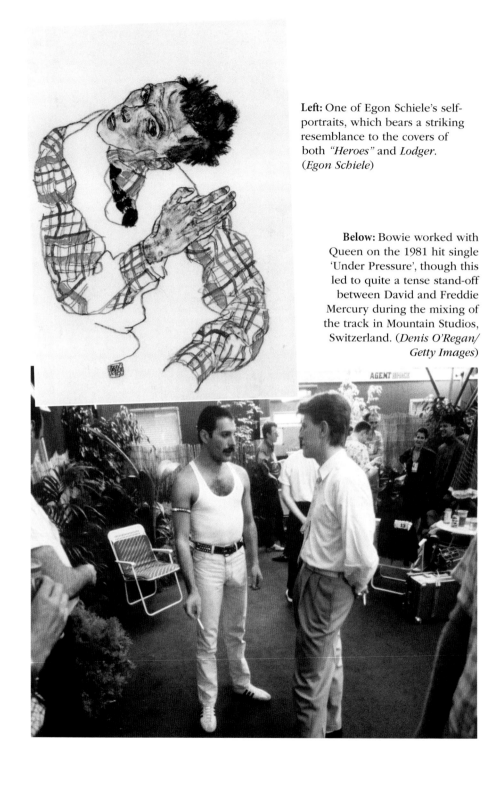

Left: One of Egon Schiele's self-portraits, which bears a striking resemblance to the covers of both *"Heroes"* and *Lodger*. (*Egon Schiele*)

Below: Bowie worked with Queen on the 1981 hit single 'Under Pressure', though this led to quite a tense stand-off between David and Freddie Mercury during the mixing of the track in Mountain Studios, Switzerland. (*Denis O'Regan/ Getty Images*)

Right: Bowie in costume as a 'Pierrot' – a clown figure from archaic Italian theatre. He was well versed in such roles as he studied mime with Lindsay Kemp, performing with him in *Pierrot In Turquoise* in 1970. (*Duffy*)

Above: An image from the video for 'Ashes To Ashes', shot on a Beach in the south of England with a cast of characters played by people lured from the London club scene.

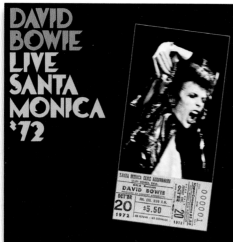

Left: The cover of the officially released live performance by Bowie & The Spiders from 1972. (*EMI*)

Right: The cadaverous and emaciated Bowie seen on the cover of the 1974 *Live* album. (*RCA*)

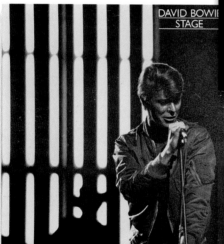

Left: Eventually, Bowie toured material from the *Low* and *"Heroes"* albums, which produced *Stage* live. (*RCA*)

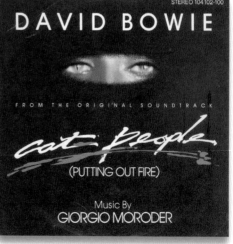

Right: Bowie's song 'Cat People' was released as a single in 1982, produced by 'disco' producer Georgio Moroder. (*RCA*)

Sane Sessions reveals an uncertain Spiders rendition, with a sleazy sax part that detracts from the urgency of the lyric.

The Mott the Hoople recording is absurdly perfect and became the anthem for the glam/glitter generation in England. People stomped to it in discos, sang it at football matches and heard it echoing down the underpass after a night on the town. It should really be credited to Bowie/Hunter, as it was Hunter's spoken word section during the fade-out (along with Mott guitarist Mick Ralphs' great riff) that helped to make the song a success. Ian Hunter said his words referred to a silly stunt they played on fans at gigs, singling someone out from the crowd, then bringing them up on stage and pouring beer over the head if they'd been throwing beer or barracking the band.

'Round And Round' (Berry)

With this Chuck Berry cover having been released on the B-side of 'Drive-In Saturday', it belongs here in spirit – another attempt at covering a classic rock song, like 'Let's Spend The Night Together'.

It's actually from the sessions for *Ziggy Stardust*, but it has the feel of the *Aladdin Sane* album with its story of a party (like 'Watch That Man') and Chuck Berry's character who is drunk and disorderly, dancing and carousing through the night. It could've been a glam anthem, but The Spiders seem a little under the weather themselves on this take. Too many parties? It was rightly considered good enough only for a B-side, the production also seeming to bury some of the playing under a sheen of anonymity.

Pin Ups (1973)

Personnel:
David Bowie: vocals, guitar, tenor and alto saxophone, harmonica, backing vocals, Moog synthesiser, arrangements
Mick Ronson: guitar, piano, vocals, arrangements
Trevor Bolder: bass
Aynsley Dunbar: drums
Mike Garson: piano, organ, harpsichord, electric piano
Ken Fordham: baritone sax
G. A. MacCormack: backing vocals
Michael Ripoche: violin
Producer: David Bowie
Running time: 33:42
Studio: Chateau d'Herouville, France (July-August 1973)
Release date: 19 October 1973
Label: RCA Victor, RS 1003 (UK), RCA Victor APL1-0291 (US)
Chart position: UK: 1, US: 23

'This is the last gig we'll ever play'. The crowd gasped. Bowie bowed out of the limelight. He really threw the cat amongst the pigeons with this statement at the Hammersmith Odeon on 3 July 1973 at the end of the last *Ziggy Stardust* concert. Kate Bush was in the audience, just as aghast as the rest of the pop world. The whole concert had been filmed. At the time, fans were confused and openly wept. Was he really saying he would never perform again? What would happen to the band? Indeed, the band were thinking as much themselves. What was going on? The answer is he was going to take a little break without telling the band (except maybe for Mick Ronson). Whilst thinking about his future, he was going to make an album of lovingly crafted covers from bands he followed when he was an up-and-coming mod in the mid-1960s. This means he definitely wasn't giving up on music, which was good news. But had he bowed out of live performance? Everyone waited with bated breath.

Thus, he retired to the Château d'Hérouville in the south of France – previously used by his mate Marc Bolan, who recorded his album *The Slider* there – and began having a ball with some of the Spiders and a few other musicians, playing some of the best sax he ever played, and turning some slices of 1960s pop and psychedelia into weirdly melodramatic glam anthems.

'Rosalyn' (Duncan, Farley)
Originally a single by The Pretty Things, this song bears a comparison to John Lennon's 'You Can't Do That' from The Beatles' *A Hard Days Night* album – both songs express jealousy and distrust towards the object of their affections. The girl in question is unreliable, and the singer is not convinced

of her chastity. With an aggressive and extremely percussive rhythm, the song opens *Pin Ups* with quite an adrenaline charge.

Bowie's strident vocal includes many tics eccentricities such as the catch in his voice at the end of the line 'Do you love me true?'. This will be one of the many joys of this album, as without his own more complex and nuanced lyrics, David gives free rein to vocal embellishments, his voice imposing and, at times, a little crazed. The other feature of this track is the drum fills from new drummer Aynsley Dunbar (a drummer with an impeccable pedigree, having played with Frank Zappa, The Jeff Beck Group and John Mayall's Bluesbreakers) that give light and shade to the mostly incessant and unrelenting rhythm track.

'Here Comes The Night' (Berns)

If you thought the prior song was in your face, this one really goes for the jugular. It starts with Ronno scratching a pick down the fretboard, followed by Bowie's rather distressing howl, leading into Ronson's fantastically accentuated no-holds-barred guitar riff joined by Bowie's sax. It sends shivers up the spine and may incur a fight-or-flight response in an unwary listener.

'Here Comes The Night' was originally a hit in 1964 for the hugely inspiring and combative performer Van Morrison and his band Them. As with 'Rosalyn', the singer has been deprived of his significant other by some other guy, and therefore, the coming of the night has all sorts of negative connotations. Bowie conveys the song with such extreme fear and anxiety, his voice like a blowtorch amidst the choppy rhythms and superb sax/guitar onslaught. Even the Hammond organ in the verses only makes the proceedings more spooky.

'I Wish You Would' (Arnold)

A theme is emerging here. The singer pleads and begs for his woman to come back. 'I won't mistreat you for no one else' is the promise, as if that made any sense. But the narrator is caught in the eternal triangle: 'Trying to love me and another man too'. The disturbing turmoil only makes the vocal sound even more anxious and delirious. Again, Ronno's guitar riff is magisterial, and the whole thing sounds quite deranged, definitely as if the singer is at the end of his tether.

This cover of a 1955 blues single by Billy Boy Arnold was an indication of David's abiding love of the original sonic template of the blues.

The album's first three songs are an amalgamation of every frustration Bowie has ever had in past relationships, maybe in his long 1960s quest for success with his many mod bands and failed singles. An electric violin plays a solo in the final part, making a big deal of itself and representing the jaundiced feelings of its narrator.

'See Emily Play' (Barrett)

With this update of a song that gives vent to something of Bowie's own existential feelings, he piles on the weirdness, as vari-speed effects alter his vocal so much that he sounds like a crazed zombie. The heavy Ronson guitar chords fall like a guillotine, and the avant-garde synth sounds from the classically trained Mike Garson sound like looming storm clouds.

With Syd Barrett's old Pink Floyd song, David is reminding us that he isn't the only writer who deals with alienation, oddness and *ennui*. Syd's missive to Emily is meant to unhinge the mind and give us entry into another world – the life of the outsider artist, the rebel poet, the maverick and the muse, though the prosaic reason for its writing was as a theme for the 'Games For May' event, a 1967 rock concert in London. It's hard not to see how Bowie saw himself in the song, and his brother Terry's schizophrenia, and, in fact, a whole panoply of artists on the edge – Dylan in the turbulent mid-1960s, Hendrix as his life unravelled in 1970, Pete Townsend with his fears and insecurities, the Rolling Stones' Keith Richards with his spiralling drug use, and even Marc Bolan with his many eccentricities. It's a paean to the crazed, the followers of Dionysus, those trying to escape the matrix, with the Devil's fiddles carving out a path through the jagged coda, redolent of the scherzo from Mahler's 4th symphony.

'Everything's Alright' (Crouch, Conrad, Stavely, James, Karlson)
Back to earth with a bump. Originally a hit for one-hit wonders The Mojos (whom Aynsley Dunbar made his name with), this is a kind of backhanded insistence on the normality of existence in the face of the strangeness and anxiety of the previous songs. Judged against the strained and emotional vocals on most of the album, it would be difficult to argue that everything was in any way 'alright'. This interpretation – probably sung slightly tongue-in-cheek – best enjoyed for its superbly arch backing vocal, is one of the most straightforward covers here.

'I Can't Explain' (Townshend)
With this memorable and instantly recognisable riff, later borrowed by the Clash for their song 'Clash City Rockers', we return to the anxious and uncertain ground that prevails for most of *Pin Ups*. Again, the 1960s drug predilection comes to mind – the LSD, cocaine, black bombers (amphetamines) and all those other little helpers that were to fuel much of the all-night dancing and endless gigging. As with Roger Daltrey's stutter on The Who's 'My Generation', there's some suggestion that the inability of the singer to speak or even make sense of his situation may be a result of the pills he's popped, although this is just one suggested reason for the stutter in 'My Generation'.

The mixture of sax and guitar is again a superb melding of instruments, as an expressive sax from Bowie leads to a dextrous Ronson guitar solo. The track being slower than the original, and the vocal a druggy drawl, it belongs in the realms of the 1960s strangeness we've already seen in 'See Emily Play'.

'Friday On My Mind' (Young, Vanda)

Originally a hit for The Easybeats in 1966, this is graced by some of David's most mannered and extraordinary phrasing. His enunciation of words like 'city' and 'pretty' is priceless, as if he's really mangling the sounds to give all the words extra excitement.

The track is a straight-ahead rocker, with baritone saxophone used for emphasis in the second chorus. But it's the vocals that *make* the song – the grumbling, sniffy 'There is nothing else that bugs me more than working for the rich man' sounds like the realistic voice of the disenfranchised wage slave. The ending has Bowie singing indistinct phrases over the backing. The backing vocals are the icing on the cake, especially the recurring 'Zoom, zoom, zoom, zoom' and 'Poor man, beggar man, thief'.

This is one of those perennial rock themes – hatred of the nine-to-five working life: something Bowie obviously felt strongly about. He mentioned in a *Russell Harty Show* interview in 1973 that while supporting the family dominated people's lives in the early 20th century, finding yourself and creating your personality/identity was now much more important.

'Sorrow' (Gottehrer, Goldstein, Feldman)

This track was a hit in the UK and was obviously constructed very carefully, its string section and sax parts carefully balanced to create quite a confection of sound. Garson's understated tremolo piano underpins the whole thing. Bowie gives it a double lead vocal, singing higher harmonies. It is not the only thing that is doubled because two saxes compete in the solo, similar to a call-and-response duel, which is quite breathtaking in its audacity. A solo cello also adds an extra note of sadness to the sorrowful sound.

One wonders if it's still David's break up with Hermione that he uses here to make the emotions of the song so touching, even though that was back in 1969. Either way, this version of the old 1960s single by both The McCoys and The Merseys is a lovely ode to lost love, played to perfection.

'Don't Bring Me Down' (Dee)

Another cover of a single originally released by The Pretty Things, their follow-up record to the previous cover on *Pin Ups*, 'Rosalyn'. Even the name of the band eventually featured in not one but two of David's songs in the future ('Pretty Thing' on Tin Machine's 1989 album and 'The Pretty Things Are Going To Hell' on *...Hours...* (1999)). As a songwriter, he is drawn to the band, whose magnum opus, *SF Sorrow*, is the kind of sci-fi concept album that Bowie himself aspires to.

The lyric is full of hip, offhand put-downs directed at people who are not on the singer's wavelength. This is accompanied by a bluesy riff, which is mutated and extended as Ronson produces a dirty, long, bent note at the end of each verse line that gives just the right amount of grit to the disenchanted narrator's unhappy lines about his untrustworthy woman. Each pre-chorus kicks in with

69

some gusto, the band rocking out into the chorus, which mirrors the stuttering rhythm of the first part of the verses. The lyrics not only describe an unfaithful girlfriend but also refer to touring: 'I even go from town to town'. This is no surprise, as its writer, Johnny Dee, not only played in The Pretty Things but had been the road manager for the rock band The Fairies.

'Shapes Of Things' (Samwell-Smith, McCarty, Relf)
This is a science-fiction parable with military drums and futuristic-sounding effects, as well as Moog synthesiser. The phrasing of certain words is again a curiosity, though Bowie's friend Geoff McCormack wrote in his autobiography that he and David would spend hours admiring and trying to imitate such inimitable vocal stylists as James Brown and Frank Sinatra. By this point, Bowie's ability to twist words into strange sounds was expert and considered.

The song was originally by The Yardbirds – a hotbed of talented guitarists, having included Jeff Beck, Jimmy Page and Eric Clapton in its ranks at some stage, so it almost begs for some exciting guitar playing, and Ronson does not disappoint, contributing a jagged, crazy solo. Bowie contributes a squeaky, angular sax part. The track is again carefully structured and ends with big power-pop chords in a shaking, shifting slow-motion collapse.

The song and its apocalyptic fears – 'Will time make man more wise?' – would've been irresistible to Bowie: wasn't this his specialist territory? But he wasn't the only one with such fears, as one his glam contemporaries, Slade, covered the similarly themed 'The Shape Of Things To Come', which they took from the 1968 film *Wild In The Streets*. But Bowie's cover of 'Shapes Of Things' is a good deal more arty.

'Anyway, Anyhow, Anywhere' (Townshend, Daltrey)
This song by The Who pushes the drums of Anysley Dunbar out into the stratosphere, trying to recreate something of the mayhem of Keith Moon's outrageous style in an extended solo section. But it's Bowie's aggressive lead vocal that brings out hidden lyric nuances. 'I can do anything!' he shouts at one point, 'Anywhere I choose!'. It sounds like a spell incantation, Bowie's mantra for his life that he would plough ahead on his quest for new musical styles and for some sort of enlightenment. He no longer needs the help of others ('do it myself!', David repeatedly whispers in an aside toward the end of the song) and he really relishes lines like, 'Nothing gets in my way/Not even locked doors'. It is truly an ode to artistic freedom, the licence to roam that touring brings, and the presumed sexual liberation that comes with stardom.

'Where Have All The Good Times Gone?' (Davies)
Here, Ronson outdoes even Dave Davies' power chords in The Kinks' original version, giving the song a heavier yet clearer rhythm guitar with a

swaying melodic line that seesaws under the swooning vocal. If anything, this is just The Kinks writ large, with even Garson's drunken barroom piano binge like the original, only more so. The whole thing could be a deranged pub singer in the back of the Clissold Arms in Finchley, doing a mad karaoke of a Kinks song.

And why would Bowie join Ray Davies in bemoaning the loss of some lost golden age? For him, it was the loss of the 1960s dream of some ideal future that he was singing about, which The Kinks, as much as The Beatles or The Stones or Dylan, represented – even though Davies was missing even earlier times when he sang the same song, an age he knew had been lost forever, an idyllic 1950s pastoral scene in which a village green was some sort of vision of innocence lost.

Outtakes/B-sides/Sessions
'Amsterdam' (Brel, Schuman)
Released as the B-side to 'Sorrow', this song was a theatrical party piece for Bowie, very similar to the song 'My Death' that he sang in his final concert as Ziggy amid hysteria from his doting fans. The two songs share a certain seriousness, with the harshness of life being brought into full focus, played simply on acoustic guitar. It's really a litany of grotesque descriptions of life as a sailor, with full force given in the vocal with its lines about debauchery and cruelty that are quite visceral: 'You can see sailors dance/ Paunches bursting their pants/Grinding women to porch'. It shows Bowie's relentless search for the evocative and the sometimes shocking in his work and performance. It also shows his love not only for Jacques Brel (a Belgian singer and actor who was a master of the French chanson tradition) but also for Scott Walker's operatic vocal style. His 1960s hits with The Walker Brothers had huge gravitas, and he also loved Brel, covering many of his songs.

'Growin' Up' (Springsteen)
This is more of an elaborate jam session than any kind of finished performance. However, as an example of how enamoured David was with Springsteen's first album *Greetings From Asbury Park*, this track was a worthwhile inclusion on the 1993 Rykodisc *Pin Ups* CD edition. With a relaxed count-in indicating that this is a tentative rehearsal take or practice session, Bowie launches into a hoarse reinvention of what Bruce wrote as an evocation of the rebellion of his attempts to circumvent the horrendous Catholic school regime. What it becomes in Bowie's hands is something else entirely: an expression of rebellion against *everything*.

The backing is barely in place by the end of the song, with Garson holding his own against the jazz piano of David Sancious' original, with Ronson's guitar part quite tentative and graceful. It's a pity this wasn't finished for release.

After *Pin Ups* had been completed, Bowie had more covers he was interested in recording and decided to make an album with his group of backing singers The Astronettes. They'd been backing him at a television show he'd made (only broadcast in America) called *The 1980 Floor Show*, filmed at London's Marquee Club in autumn 1973, in which he performed songs from *Pin Ups* and *Aladdin Sane* and several songs from the forthcoming *Diamond Dogs*. The three backing singers were Ava Cherry (with whom he was romantically involved), his best friend from school days, Geoff MacCormack, and a second male singer, Jason Guest. Twelve songs were recorded for a prospective Astronettes album, on which Bowie played several instruments, wrote six songs himself and produced. It was released on CD in the 2000s in two different unauthorised versions, the most recent being *The Astronettes Sessions*, on the Black Barbarella label, simply credited to Ava Cherry.

'I Am A Laser' (Bowie)
This starts with funky rhythm guitar, presaging '1984' on the subsequent album *Diamond Dogs*. A lot of the tracks around this time reflect Bowie's newfound interest in soul/disco music, which had begun its inexorable rise to cultural dominance as the seventies wore on. Ava Cherry's vocal is rich and full, with the required soulful sound to bring the track to life. Though none of these tracks were released officially, this one was good enough for David to return to during sessions for his own soul-influenced album, *Young Americans*, where he taped his own vocal (which can be found online). Even later, the song was completely rewritten and became 'Scream Like A Baby' on *Scary Monsters (And Super Creeps)*.

'Seven Days' (Peacock)
What sounds like a Mick Ronson guitar part embellishes the introduction to this song by Annette Peacock – a Moog synthesiser pioneer who was on the same label as Bowie: RCA. Again, Cherry sings the ballad in a soul style, with a bluesy edge, in a very simple arrangement. Interestingly, it's not widely known that Mick Ronson wrote his own song called 'Life On Mars', which was very much like this song: almost identical in feel, especially the guitar parts.

'God Only Knows' (Wilson, Asher)
Eventually covered by Bowie in a more-stripped-down arrangement on the 1984 *Tonight* album, this magisterial Beach Boys classic is given a soul makeover with a nuanced Ava Cherry lead vocal. Dressed in a lovely Tony Visconti arrangement sometime after the original session, this has saxophones and mandolins, very similar to Visconti's arrangement of George Harrison's 'Try Some, Buy Some' on Bowie's 2003 album *Reality*. Recorder harmonies cascade over occasional delicate piano and a lively saxophone solo is the high point.

'Having A Good Time' (Bowie)
The first track on the album featuring the two male singers strongly resembles the sound of The Beach Boys' *Holland* album. The lyric is an encouragement to hedonistic excess, like several disco songs of the era. A softly sensuous, gently rippling tremolo-Wurlitzer electric piano dominates the mix, with a languidly descending chord sequence like The Troggs' 'Love Is All Around'. After a false ending, the song reignites with an even stronger male vocal part, giving it a powerhouse conclusion.

'People From Bad Homes' (Bowie)
This title eventually became part of the lyric for 'Fashion' on *Scary Monsters*, but the rest of the lyric only confuses the listener. The chorus seems critical of the people in question: 'People of notions play out this game'; 'People of caution have trouble in love'. The verses are sung by Cherry, with the two male vocalists taking the chorus. This is full-to-brimming with Bowie's supremely slovenly and louche saxophone: quite a delight! It's another soul song, with Cherry's breathy whispering adding a little extra sensuality to the final bars.

'Highway Blues' (Harper)
Bowie was a great admirer of English singer-songwriter Roy Harper and they were contemporaries in the days of the Beckenham Arts Lab, where they were both building a small following playing to folk club crowds. Harper's oeuvre is replete with diatribes against civilisation and gentle folky ballads, all of which made their mark on David in the early days. A good candidate to be the English Bob Dylan, Harper went electric and produced the three fine masterpieces *HQ*, *Bullinamingvase* and *Unknown Soldier* in the late 1970s, but he never made the big time.

'Highway Blues' (originally from Harper's quirky 1973 album *Lifemask*) has vocals from Cherry, MacCormack and Guest. The chorus rhythm has confusing bars of 7/8, which almost derails the song, but it finds greater urgency as more percussion and drums push it ahead. At the beginning, Bowie is heard calling out the chord 'C!', possibly in a fit of desperation. The two male leads sing it less confidently, and it improves every time Cherry's vocal comes in.

'Only Me' (Bowie)
Another soul-style ballad – a progenitor of 'It's Gonna Be Me' – and coincidentally also a rejected song from the later *Young Americans* sessions. A soft hesitancy in the male lead vocal is at times disconcerting, and the lyric is generic middle-of-the-road stuff, the singer deserted by a lover and trying to cajole them into coming back: 'What have you got to lose, only me?' A swirling Hammond organ part becomes the dominant instrument right at the end, lifting the track, and one wonders why this was not deployed earlier, as along with the simple guitar runs, the fadeout is the best part.

'Things To Do' (Bowie)
Masterful rhythms from Aynsley Dunbar kick off this track, which has a
sneaky guitar riff, powerful bass from Herbie Flowers and great piano
pulses from Garson. There are stuttering rhythm-guitar chords, with all three
vocalists singing together, sounding a little like Jefferson Airplane. The lyrics
are laughably insubstantial ('I love you, you, you/I got things to do, do, do'),
but there are a number of religious references, implying that Bowie may have
intended this to be a gospel number: St. Peter and the Lord himself being
mentioned amongst other Biblical personages. After an unfinished passage
with Latin rhythms possibly awaiting a solo, we hear Bowie count in the last
verse.

'How Could I Be Such A Fool' (Frank Zappa)
Frank Zappa was a towering figure in US counterculture, especially in the late
1960s and early 1970s. He was not only a songwriter of extraordinary ability
(check out 'Inca Roads' from *One Size Fits All*) but also a virtuoso guitarist
with dextrous ability on the fretboard and a sound and style to rival Hendrix.
He also arranged and produced a multiplicity of albums in various genres,
including avant-garde jazz, musique concrete, orchestral, rock, pop and doo-
wop. His singing voice and often outrageous lyrics are still an acquired taste.
   This song from the first Mothers Of Invention album *Freak Out!* is a big
production similar in style to the prior 'God Only Knows', with mandolins
and saxophones to the fore. The male vocal (no clear credits have emerged to
say whether Guest or Maccormack) does sound as if it was, to some extent,
emulating Zappa's lugubrious tones. Ava Cherry's voice is very low in the
mix, as are the harp glissandos towards the end.

'I'm In The Mood For Love' (Mackintosh, Fields)
This old standard from the 1935 film *Every Night At Eight* is the least
appealing of all the Astronettes tracks as it's muddled and messy. Bowie's
arrangement attempts to place a misguided, quick-fire, rap-like vocal over
the Ava Cherry lead vocal, with terrible results. Neither the cool lead nor the
panicky-sounding rap can be clearly discerned. What gives? The jabbering
male vocals give the song a silly show-tune feel. To heap ignominy on an
already over-egged cake, Bowie then throws in several cheesy synth shrieks,
only relenting at the fade.

'Spirits In The Night' (Bruce Springsteen)
No one would've expected Bowie to have attempted another Springsteen
cover, given that the primary drive behind this album appeared to be to
produce futuristic soul/disco music.
   Unfortunately, lead vocalist Jason Guest is prone to adding melodramatic
insinuations into the lyrics, giving the song a similarly sickly feel to 'I'm
In The Mood for Love'. The song becomes another show tune and not the

soul ballad Bowie no doubt had in mind, and it's clear why he realised that The Astronettes couldn't do what he wanted them to. The lead vocal is very macho and is not helped by Cherry's doo-wop backing vocals.

A rock/R&B section comes to an abrupt halt, leading into the final verse, as did Springsteen's live version of the song at the time, though his was full of real emotion.

'I Am Divine' (Bowie)

This funky gospel piece has Bowie's fingerprints all over it: 'So you think I dress to impress you?'. It is very much in the style of the future *Young Americans* tracks, with a string section including pizzicato violin parts. The lyrics are exuberant and laughably egotistical – 'I walk a fine line' we are told, ''cause I'm so divine'. The male lead voice is a long way from the main man, but it still holds its own. As the song progresses, there's a fine-pumping bass line from Herbie Flowers and some fancy, funky guitar from Bowie and Mark Carr-Pritchard. In the end, the piano part becomes a little unhinged in the style of 'Aladdin Sane', intriguingly equating divinity with some form of madness.

Diamond Dogs (1974)

Personnel:
David Bowie: vocals, backing vocals, guitar, keyboards, harmonica, saxophone
Mike Garson: piano, keyboards
Herbie Flowers: bass
Aynsley Dunbar, Tony Newman: drums
Alan Parker: guitar ('1984')
Producer: David Bowie
Running time: 38:25
Studios: Olympic, London; Ludolph, Holland (January-February 1974)
Release date: 24 May 1974
Label: RCA Victor, APL1-0576 (UK), CPL1-0576 (US)
Chart position: UK: 1, US: 5

'Strangest Living Curiosities!'. This slogan is prominent on the album cover and is a good entry point to an understanding of the whole *Diamond Dogs* concept. The slogan is next to a depiction of Bowie as a dog. The illustrator was Guy Peelaert, whose rock artworks have been anthologised many times in book form. It alludes to the idea of the travelling freak show, dime-store museums and itinerant circus performers of another age, especially in the US.

Bowie's imagination was piqued by the silent-era film *Freaks*, which is mentioned in the title track. This film was a precursor to David Cronenberg's body-horror films, depicting a troupe of deformed and disenfranchised outsiders performing town-to-town in a troubled circus. Beyond this initial inspiration, the album is a picture of a devastated post-apocalyptic city, now the mainstay of many online games and TV shows that are populated by zombies, misfits and mutants that roam the streets in gangs.

David's handwritten illustrations and ideas for stage sets depicting Hunger City still exist, and to some extent, these were brought to life on the *Diamond Dogs* tour, which was well represented on the following *David Live* album – though the lack of a complete live film of this fantastic, melodramatic theatrical performance is close to criminal.

All this came about because the widow of author George Orwell refused permission to use the ideas from his post-war novel *1984*. Many of the *Diamond Dogs* songs (most obviously '1984' and 'Big Brother') were written in an attempt to create a musical based on the book. When the rights to ideas from the book were refused, Bowie went back to the drawing board. 'I really had to turn around on a dime', he later commented.

He had secretly harboured a desire to create a rock opera or musical stage show. This album was where he finally got serious. It's also notable for his being reunited with polymath and producer Tony Visconti, who engineered the album, though it was produced by Bowie. It's also important to note that many instruments were played by David himself.

'Future Legend' (Bowie)

This piece of performance poetry is our introduction to the devastated
Hunger City, central to the album's characters, replacing the war-torn London
of Orwell's original novel. The lyrics were printed on the inside gatefold,
replicated on some cardboard CD reissues over a vaguely sepia-tinted
multiple-image of a fog-bound urban sprawl.

'The last few corpses lay rotting on the slimy thoroughfare' is a good
impression of what to expect from this evocation of post-apocalyptic urban
decay. The musical background is a smorgasbord of sinister, childlike zombie
voices intoning indecipherable nonsense, with a bed of synth sounds and
distorted guitar. That the track apparently quotes from the 1940 Rogers and
Hammerstein show song 'Bewitched, Bothered And Bewildered' is the icing
on the cake in terms of David's ironic sense of humour.

'Diamond Dogs' (Bowie)

The title track bursts forth from the poisonous smog of 'Future Legend',
big and brash with an old-fashioned, no-holds-barred rumble – David
declaring, 'This ain't rock 'n' roll, this is ... genocide!'. The style template
is the Chicago blues via The Rolling Stones and The Yardbirds, dominated
by floor toms and a luscious saxophone over David's startling, glammed-up
guitar rhythm.

The lyric depicts 'Halloween Jack' – which some have taken to be David's
persona on this album – sliding down a rope onto the wrecked streets like
Tarzan to join one of the many mutant gangs that roam there. It's not a fun
place to be, but there is something of a tarnished splendour to be had from
the purloined jewels the characters sport: 'Her face is *sans* feature, but she
wears a Dali brooch'. Pollution is a serious issue, though, as Bowie advises of
the smog-like poisonous mist in Hunger City: 'Come out of the garden baby/
You'll catch your death in the fog'.

But why was Bowie interested in this sort of situation? Why the broken
city? Why the name 'Diamond Dogs'? It's easy to forget that for him and
his friend Marc Bolan, the London of childhood was very much Orwell's
bombed-out, post-war scenario. It would've held a fascination for Bowie,
just because the dark streets Winston Smith walks in *1984* (and in the later
1984 movie version made in England (with a Eurythmics soundtrack inspired
by Bowie) are the streets from Bowie's own past. The idea of a gang called
Diamond Dogs is easily arrived at if you see the two images as representative
of two different ends of his conceptual framework: diamonds at the top of the
social scale and dogs at the bottom. It's a meeting of opposites, an impossible
conglomeration. The freaks, outcasts and misfits are just a reflection of the
sexual ambivalence of the early 1970s, David's association with Lou Reed
while producing his *Transformer* album, and the weirdly camp glam scene
they helped to create, reflected in the characters from Lou's big song 'Walk
On The Wild Side'.

'Sweet Thing' (Bowie)

The song fades in with jumbled backwards piano and guitar and resolves into a stately ballad, with emphasis on the end of each line from distorted guitar and, later, mournful saxophone. 'Sweet Thing' is sung from the point of view of a politician's lover – the politician who is the centrepiece of the next track 'Candidate'. There's a sense of uncertainty in the lines 'I'm glad that you're older than me/Makes me feel important and free'.

As the song proceeds, more Mike Garson piano trills intrude on the melody, giving a more decadent and sumptuous edge to the tune. This eventually leads to a tasteful guitar solo by David, who'd obviously been paying attention when Mick Ronson had performed similar duties on earlier albums. The solo is beautifully plangent, leading into the next song, which is a continuation of the same theme – the whole thing is sometimes presented as one song: 'Sweet Thing/Candidate/Sweet Thing'.

Interestingly, this three-song suite began as a much more uptempo tune with the simple title, 'Candidate' (a demo is available on some older CD issues), but when Bowie found he had to restyle the whole thing to remove obvious references to the Orwell novel, 'Sweet Thing' was added as both the intro and conclusion. It makes the song more dramatic and bookends it nicely, framing the 'Candidate' section as if it were a movie with a tragic ending, the 'Sweet Thing' section gently commenting on it: 'hope, boys, is a cheap thing'.

'Candidate' (Bowie)

The piece lurches into existence out of the ruins of the previous track, giving a sense of the politician and his lover beginning a long walk together. The sense of pervading doom created by the lush chords and sorrowful saxophone is all-enveloping and paints a picture of a dead-end excursion: 'My set is amazing, it even smells like a street'. But this is no happy ending, for it concludes with 'We'll buy some drugs ... then jump in the river'.

The slow, inexorable sonorities of this tale of trouble show David's definite dislike for what he'd experienced of US politics, having by now seen the squeaky-clean TV ads enough times to be repulsed by their cheerful vacuity. In this song, there are all the signs of everyman's disillusion with the era of Nixon and the loss of innocence that went with the string of political assassinations that included both the Kennedy brothers and Martin Luther King. It's a story that offers 'bulletproof faces: Charlie Manson, Cassius Clay', implying that fame in America might lead to assassination. It's a litany of 'poisonous people/Spreading rumours and lies and stories they made up'.

'Sweet Thing (Reprise)' (Bowie)

One long saxophone wail reintroduces the original song and the question, 'Do you think that your face looks the same?' When the song finally surges to its conclusion, the piano, sax and guitars are met with a Mellotron flute part that really does feel like a 'snowstorm freezing your brain'. But it's a beautifully musical maelstrom as if cocooning the two characters, who are protected by their hope of 'a street with a deal'. Then there's a musical coda that's like the sound of machinery – the massive media machine that chews up hopeful politicians (and their equally hopeful lovers) and then spits them out – as the deadly distortion-saturated chords come to a sudden halt.

'Rebel Rebel' (Bowie)

What a riff! It's certainly one of the dirtiest, stonking humdingers of a riff ever conceived. The song stalks on that mighty guitar riff like some kinky, slinky vagabond, dragging the listener into his story of the mother who's 'in a whirl' and their offspring who is entirely sexually ambivalent. But what of the rebel? Though that could be thought to be any 1970s glam teen, there are more interesting possibilities. Looking at the song as the centrepiece of the album, could it be the *1984* character Winston Smith presented as a transvestite? More likely, it's his rebel lover Julia, someone who leads Winston further into the secret underground world of resistance to Big Brother – a rebel against the authoritarian state: that political world examined in the previous song.
  The track closes with the riff *ad infinitum,* Bowie doing his stock vocal improvisation over it – 'Got your transmission and a live wire', 'A handful of 'ludes'. The lines make sure that you understand this is a contemporary scenario and not just a futuristic stage play.

'Rock 'N' Roll With Me' (Bowie, Peace)

A collaboration with David's close friend Geoff McCormack (whom Bowie nicknamed Warren Peace), this is really part two of the album's centrepiece and can be interpreted as the culmination of the affair between Winston Smith and Julia before they are discovered and become prisoners to be indoctrinated into the totalitarian state. There is a definite feeling of lassitude and hubris in the distorted chords, lazy saxophone and the lyrics: 'A room to rent while the lizards lay, crying in the heat'. The lovers are lying in their hidden rendezvous – spent after lovemaking – and their doomed love is like a wonderful blazing torch, burning up the broken streets they live in, torching Big Brother's hateful slogans. Their love seems truly 'The door that lets me out', as Bowie sings.
  The song chorus is instantly catchy, like 'Rebel Rebel': one of two obvious singles on the album. Indeed, 1960s troubadour Donovan released a carbon copy of 'Rock 'N' Roll With Me' as a single later in 1974, though his version contained a string section, where Bowie's track is buoyed by Hammond organ.

'We Are The Dead' (Bowie)

The sound is drenched in echo and reverb as if we are drowning in a sea of troubled waters, with the obligatory electric piano and fuzz guitar leading us down treacherous sea paths at midnight, through shadowy caverns as if descending into Dante's underworld.

Still, in the twilight shade of the novel *1984*, we are here plunged into even deeper darkness, for the slogan 'We are the dead' – something Winston says to Julia – intimates that to stand against the despotic tyrant Big Brother means they have become outcasts, pariahs, and might as well be dead. It also has the accepted biblical connotation, as in when Christ advised the disciples to 'Let the dead bury the dead'. The implication is that life is nothing without freedom, without the spirit, the soul, and that life is not worth living without being able to live fully: live without the deadening duplicity of a state-controlled existence. Love, of course, is central to this idea of freedom. And for all its heavy, gloomy, drug and sex-related language, this is still a love song, sung from one character to another.

At one point, there are images of a board room – a 'theatre of financiers' – and we are suddenly catapulted into Bowie's idea of hell: a place where money is all that is of interest, and those suits around the table are 'white and dressed to kill'. The lovers are discovered, captured and forced into captivity. They are later to be reintroduced into life in the totalitarian city and won't even recognise each other: so effectively have they been re-educated.

'1984' (Bowie)

Often incorporated in concert into a medley with well-known *Diamond Dogs* outtake 'Dodo', '1984' is where Bowie first attempted a funk style. The rhythm guitar (played by Alan Parker) is in the style of 'Theme From Shaft' – the then-current Isaac Hayes hit single. '1984' also shows a James Brown influence. Bowie was to continue further down this path on the next album *Young Americans*. But this is where comparisons with that genre end, as the funky wah-wah guitar belies an extremely sinister song with a message that still resonates today.

With a swooping string section scored by Tony Visconti, the track includes a romantic bridge with a much more gentle melody and a sudden *laissez-faire* attitude from its protagonist: 'We played an all-night movie role/You said it would last'. When Parker's guitar resumes normal service with its choppy, nihilistic funk, the song returns to its sober message: a warning about the rise of totalitarianism and its accompanying militarism.

'Big Brother' (Bowie)

Beginning with a synthesiser trumpet sound and a Mellotron choir, 'Big Brother' is the big, cynical kiss-off to this monumental journey that takes you from a poisonous apocalypse to a *fait accompli* of a society drunk on its own fear and lassitude. With a mood like a debauched tearoom party piece, this ribald tongue-in-cheek track titters and sneers: 'Don't talk of dust and roses/ Or should we powder our noses?'.

Like a more authoritarian follow-up to the song 'Aladdin Sane', this depicts the infantile self-aggrandisement of the rich upper classes, wallowing in their expectation of the status quo continuing: 'We want you Big Brother'. They love the idea of being part of the ruling party, masochistic to boot: 'Someone to shame us/Some brave Apollo'. The chorus is remarkably memorable: acoustic guitars vying with saxophones and drums. Then, the synth trumpet blows its reveille-like call one more time, and, with a final flourish, we are thrown into the boneyard.

'Chant Of The Ever Circling Skeletal Family' (Bowie)
This musically circular, electric-guitar-dominated piece powers forward using all the mutated effects we've come to expect from Bowie's excellent playing on the album. Disorienting and disembodied voices like those crying in the background on 'Future Legend' keep encouraging us to 'Move it up' and 'Shake it up', on and on into oblivion. These are lost voices, voices of the dead, the complicit, or of strange spirits, like the voices at the end of that tongue-twister *Hunky Dory* closer 'The Bewley Brothers'. When you finally get sick of it, there is just one word left looping at the end: 'Run!'.

Outtakes/Demos
'Dodo' (Bowie)
David intended to insert 'Dodo' either immediately after '1984' or as a medley with that song. It was performed by him on the US TV show *The 1980 Floor Show,* recorded at London's Marquee Club in 1973.

It's a description of citizens informing on their neighbours, as is encouraged in totalitarian countries taught to fear their regimes: 'Here comes neighbour Jim, come to turn you in/Another dodo/You didn't hear it from me'. However, the track wasn't used, most likely because it was too light-hearted in tone, making the harrowing fear of one's neighbour shopping you for some perceived crime no more than a farce. The music didn't help that perception either, as it sounds somewhat like an oompah band and oddly Germanic. ('Dodo' and '1984/Dodo' are available on a number of CD reissues.)

Young Americans (1975)

Personnel:
David Bowie: vocals, guitars, keyboards
David Sanborn: saxophone
Mike Garson: piano
Carlos Alomar, Earl Slick: guitar
Luther Vandross, Ava Cherry, Robin Clark, Anthony Hinton, Diane Sumler: backing vocals
Willie Weeks: bass
Andy Newmark, Dennis Davis: drums
Ralph MacDonald, Pablo Rosario: percussion
Producers: David Bowie, Tony Visconti, Harry Maslin
Running time: 40:18
Studios: Sigma Sound, Philadelphia; Record Plant and Electric Lady, New York
Release date: 7 March 1975
Label: RCA Victor PK-11678 (UK), APL-1-0998 (US)
Chart position: UK: 2, US: 9

In the 1974 BBC documentary *Cracked Actor,* charting Bowie's arrival in America and his impact there, the interviewer asks him how he is adjusting to life in the big country, and Bowie looks slightly amused at the question. In the back of a taxi speeding through a US city, the man who was once ready to take the vows of a Buddhist monk is bent over a carton of milk, pondering his life. He answers, 'There's a fly in here, and it's soaking up a lot of milk'. He looked into the milk as he looked into all things: with the eye of a poet, an artist. Bowie was ever in thrall to his art, to his need for expression, and this gnomic comment is like a mysterious haiku.

Young Americans was influenced by Marc Bolan's previous album *Zinc Alloy And The Hidden Riders Of Tomorrow (A Creamed Cage In August)* (1974). As Marc and David were true musical sparring partners, when he saw Marc getting involved with his black T. Rex backing vocalist Gloria Jones and producing an album of soul/funk sounds with gospel backing vocals, David wanted in. *Young Americans* is an even more authentic soul album than Marc's released a year before. It's an album that brings a new commercial sheen to Bowie's canon. The instrumentation is more low-key and slinky, prominently displaying the saxophone stylings of David Sanborn, who played on the sessions in Philadelphia, the 1970s soul/disco capital. David hand-picked session musicians from the genre.

The original album title was – obscurely – *The Gouster*: a reference to black fashions in 1960s Chicago, to gangster hipness and street cool. (An album was recreated from Bowie's initial track listing with this title for the CD box set *Who Can I Be Now*, released in 2016). No doubt this had immense significance to the increasingly coked-up Bowie, but it would've simply confused his audience. Good job it occurred to him that an album title with the word 'American' in it might give it more stateside appeal, for indeed, it was so successful in that country that record executives pleaded with him to do another *Young Americans* for years afterwards.

'Young Americans' (Bowie)
Straight from the superb drum fill that opens the song, we are immediately in a whole other sound world to Bowie's previous albums. Showing the clear influence of soul, R&B, gospel and funk, this is clearly a concerted effort by Bowie, Harry Maslin and Tony Visconti to produce a kind of crossover blue-eyed soul only previously achieved by Hall & Oates on their *Abandoned Luncheonette* album (1972).

The song is a funky stew of saxophone and keyboard textures, with slick rhythm guitar from Carlos Alomar. What we have here is a song that alternates between a ballad and something that can be danced to. The lyrics have an interesting, impressionistic feel. The first two verses are sung from the point of view of two working-class young lovers, already getting into adult situations that will cause work routine or parenthood to enter their lives too soon. But the allure of physical love and the pressure to look good and experience everything immediately is overwhelming: 'You want the young American'.

The idea of the 'young American' is fleshed out more fully in verses three and four and the short bridge that begins 'Do you remember your President Nixon?'. It's almost a sociological perspective for the song's final parts, Bowie commenting on the lives of young Americans: 'Blacks got respect and whites got the soul train'. He piles up the imagery of America as he sees it incessantly. What's made abundantly clear is that he's no more immune to the pleasures of the American dream than his song's characters are.

The track builds to an absolute crescendo when the music stops and Bowie croons, 'Ain't there one damn song that can make me break down and cry?'. This plays into the album's emotional, soul/gospel-derived bedrock, and we know we are in for a wild ride. His vocal is preternaturally powerful and soulful.

'Win' (Bowie)
Much credit should be given to Luther Vandross for his fantastic vocal arrangements on the album. This is the first song that really relies on the interplay between Bowie's lead voice and the carefully placed responses from the backing singers, giving that wonderful swooping gospel support. It is a song of love, but this is undoubtedly deeply sensual love with its sweetly orgasmic major-7th chords and glissandos. 'People like you should not be allowed to start any fires', David intones playfully, and it's clear that the winning here is all about getting it on and getting what you want from a sexual encounter. From another perspective, the idea of winning is central to the whole concept of the American dream, and 'All you've got to do is win'.

83

The keyboards intertwined with the sax and crying lead guitar are absolutely magnificent, giving the song a swooning, irresistible charm, sending us off into sensual Seventh Heaven.

'Fascination' (Bowie, Vandross)

This is a much more up-tempo and funky piece, with lots of choppy rhythm guitar interplay between Earl Slick and Carlos Alomar. It is amazing how the Hendrix-like wah-wah guitar in this piece fits so fully into the soul/disco genre, having lost its association with 1960s psychedelia, largely as a result of its use by Sly Stone and Parliament/Funkadelic.

'Fascination' is much more vocally evocative, with improvised vocal ideas from Bowie and the backing singers. Again, Luther Vandross and his team are to be congratulated, the song itself being based on the Vandross song 'Funky Music (Is Part Of Me)'. This is wildly inventive rhythmically and full of gospel emotion.

The lyric focuses on an important factor of Bowie's personality, as he'd sung in 'Changes': 'Strange fascination taking over me'. He was always finding a new obsession, inspired by other art, music, costume or film, and was able to focus on these, becoming entranced by new ideas, feelings or sounds and using them for his own art. Thus the song is crucial to any understanding of Bowie's personality and music. He sings, 'Fascination takes a part of me/I can't help it/I've got to use it every time'.

'Right' (Bowie)

Footage exists of Bowie and his backing vocalists rehearsing this superb vocal arrangement, which was again meticulously crafted by Luther Vandross. The lyric was slight, almost sexually explicit, but still vague enough to slip past the censors, until one of the backing vocalists gives the game away by extemporising between the lyrics: 'Doing it, get it on'. The music is at times in the same ballpark as the closing track 'Fame', with extreme emphasis on the rhythm. But it's much calmer at the beginning, suggesting a supreme sensual serenity, with a gentle rhythm and soupy guitar chords spreading out like a sea: 'Flying such a sweet placing/Coming inside and safe'.

The call-and-response gospel vocals that close the song are so intricate and fine that one can get caught up in singing along, forced to compete with what amounts to a perfect musical confection, impossible to repeat exactly. It builds and builds, reminding us that there's 'Never no turning back'.

'Somebody Up There Likes Me' (Bowie)

A throwback to *Diamond Dogs*, this song is about media stars (such as himself), though the focus seems to be on politicians: 'Hugging all the babies/Kissing all the ladies'. The lyric tells us to beware of these interlopers into our daily existence – decrying the power of television, pop idols and advertisers, complaining that 'When we were young, any man was judged by what he'd done/But now you pick them on the screen'.

The music is doom-laden, in keeping with the mood of *Diamond Dogs* which had its own track about a candidate. But this one is much more open-ended in its condemnation of media culture figures, Bowie positioning himself in the discourse, for can he be trusted any more than a politician or an advertiser? He, too, has something to sell. And the time to trust him least is when he reassuringly tells us, 'Don't worry, baby/Somebody up there likes me'. Divine providence can be claimed by politicians and pop stars alike.

'Across The Universe' (Lennon, McCartney)

Just as *Aladdin Sane* had its Rolling Stones cover song, *Young Americans* has this Beatles song, though the song was entirely written by John Lennon. It's said that *Young Americans* was already complete without this track or 'Fame' being included. Instead, there were at least three other possible tracks, which are considered at the end of this chapter.

However, after that first version of the album was ready and Tony Visconti had left for his next production job, Bowie bumped into John Lennon in the studio. At first, wary of each other's reputations and fame, the two eventually hit it off to the extent of recording this reverent treatment of the lovely Lennon song and, of course, collaborating on what became their hit song 'Fame'. Visconti was later disappointed when discovering he'd missed this great meeting of musical minds and wished David had called him to oversee the session. Many might have been surprised that The Beatles' esoteric ballad had been so successfully transformed with a soul sound, but the musicianship is again exemplary: in particular, the guitar figure that enhances the melody beautifully. Bowie delivers a powerhouse vocal in the chorus, emotionally reconstructing a song that was originally fairly lethargic and placid.

'Can You Hear Me' (Bowie)

Perhaps the most beautiful and uplifting Bowie love song, this is almost hypnotic and features a truly heartfelt vocal from the main man. In fact, every detail of this skeletal track is finely wrought – the opening reverb-enhanced chords, the soaring string line that lifts us into the stratosphere, the wailing saxophone, but most of all, the syrupy, sweet-as-molasses background vocals that support Bowie's impassioned words.

The lyrics are again heavily sexual (including the double meaning 'Can you feel me inside?') and effortlessly evoke the beginnings of a physical relationship: a feeling almost transcendent in its absolute joy. Here, David pours on the honey, making this a more heavily sensual and sensitive song than he'd ever attempted previously. 'Sexual Healing' and 'Let's Get It On' by Marvin Gaye provided an obvious template, though the songs of Barry White also act as a recent inspiration for this sound.

'Fame' (Bowie, Lennon, Alomar)

Derived from jamming on a song by The Flares that Carlos Alomar liked called 'Footstompin'', Lennon and Bowie soon had a nice little song that sought to encapsulate their experiences as media celebrities, with all the pitfalls. Alomar's riff brings the track to life with its intricate clipped notes, allied to that conclusive four-note burst of sound at the end of each line.

The track was made to dance to, being quite propulsive rhythmically, but has many tricks and idiosyncrasies, such as the machine-gun drum fills, the high falsetto vocal lines Bowie throws in, and the much-celebrated speeding up and slowing down of his and Lennon's voices as they repeatedly sing the word 'fame'. Lennon and Bowie colluded on the vocal parts, with their voices beginning high – an intimation of the highlife, the high wire, being high on drugs, etc. – before plunging into the lowest of tones, depicting the artist's slow descent in the pitfalls of fame itself, as if they are being sucked down into the mire of complacency. The telling line is certainly 'What you want is in the limo', for indeed, there was the drink, drugs, groupies and the restless, constant travel that Bowie desired. As already mentioned, this was something of a downward spiral for him, and this track, above all else, gives the lie to the common perception of stardom being a bed of roses. It's not in evidence here – just a comment on the breathless, exhaustive search for the next high, the next hit, the next affair, the next look and the next place.

Outtakes/Bonus Tracks
'Who Can I Be Now?' (Bowie)

This is available on the 2003 CD reissue and in the *Sound And Vision* box set. The sound is anthemic and commercial, carried along by the usual stew of sax and backing voices, this time underscored by piano. It could've been another 'All The Young Dudes', another signature song for David, the well-known chameleon of rock, who changed personality as easily as he changed his clothes.

'Who Can I Be Now?' is about identity, the difficulty of staying ahead of the curve, and how deeply influences go into the psyche. If any track originally recorded for this album had a gospel influence specifically, it's this one. 'Everybody's raised in blindness' could be the opening line of any spiritually uplifting gospel song played in any church in the land. And, of course, the impact of the word of the Lord is always meant to radically alter the personality for its adherents to be born again. But the real question for Bowie at the end of it all is, 'Can I be real?'.

Even more interestingly, this is not the only additional song with gospel underpinnings, for Bowie's next album, *Station To Station,* was to hold his most explicitly religious song yet: 'Word On A Wing'.

It seems that as he struggled more and more visibly with his addiction to cocaine and other stimulants, he was really searching and seeking spiritually, hoping for salvation, and trying, in his confused and disturbed mental state, to find release.

'After Today' (Bowie)
Found in the *Sound And Vision* box set, this is a celebratory song in which the singer is exhilarated by some new life event to the extent that he feels completely free. Maybe he's met someone new, or it could be something else. In my own sci-fi novel *Critical Mass*, I used the song in a chapter denoting how the world changes after aliens first arrive on Earth.

Starting with a big drum intro kicking in like James Brown's rhythm section, we have a lively, funky rhythm guitar interpolated with a bass line and piano figure that keeps the song moving along compulsively. 'After today, fortune, man, will find you'. Bowie is breathless in his excitement, as whatever has occurred (maybe another 'strange fascination' he's caught onto in his new adopted home) may be another American author who has gotten into Bowie's head as William Burroughs and Jack Kerouac did. But the suggestion again may be that he's been caught up in some spiritual fervour, some esoteric work, for it is well known that he was still interested in Nietzsche and the *Kabbalah* – a work of religious scholarship that can be powerful and diverting stuff, even to an expert on mysticism and the occult. These interests were to come to the fore in his next recordings: truly both a zenith and a nadir for him.

'It's Gonna Be Me' (Bowie)
This ballad is an epic, as soulful and emotional as anything David ever attempted, on a par with 'Wild Is The Wind', but from his own pen. Nothing can prepare you for the serious attitude: there isn't really anything else like it. Unlike other epics like 'Time' or 'Life On Mars?', this is an intimate portrait of the artist as a young lover in the throes of tragic innocence. And perhaps that is the key – this is too revealing, tries too hard to be *real*, and instead shows the level of Bowie's artifice. The emotion is just a little too keen, the lyric too complex to tell the story of any true romance.

The skeletal, piano-led arrangement (fully realised in Tony Visconti's string arrangement on the 2003 CD release) is halting and sensitive, with peaks and troughs building to a series of climaxes, with Bowie's voice teasing and cajoling, trying to convince us of his depth of feeling. But in the end, it's not convincing, as even in the beauty of its arrangement and the passion of the vocal performance, it is flawed. Bowie's emotional life has not yet allowed him to convey deep feelings about human relationships convincingly, but he would get much closer to it with 'Wild Is The Wind' on the next album.

'John, I'm Only Dancing (Again)' (Bowie)
Though Bowie created this clunky dance track at the *Young Americans* sessions and eventually released it as a single in 1979, it's clear he didn't

think it was that important in 1975. It's a silly, slight lyric, almost as ludicrous as Bob Dylan's 'Country Pie' on *Nashville Skyline* when he was attempting to reinvent himself as a country crooner – both of the greatest songwriters of the 20th century producing laughable doggerel in the name of change – Dylan with his 'he's got that hogshead up on his toe', David with 'Jumping John, the great goose is gone'.

This disco update is not a patch on the original 'John, I'm Only Dancing' single from the Ziggy period, but it's a lot of fun, with an arrangement full of tricky beats and little considered guitar parts, giving it character and commercial credibility. The horn section alone is worth the price of admission. As disco took over from glam rock, this ability to create dance-floor filler was to put David in the driving seat. He was always capable of producing songs you wanted to dance to in addition to the serious stuff.

Station To Station (1976)

David Bowie: vocals, guitar, keyboards, harmonica, saxophone, Moog, Mellotron, backing vocals
Roy Bittan: piano, organ
Carlos Alomar, Earl Slick: guitar
George Murray: bass
Dennis Davis: drums
Warren Peace: backing vocals, percussion
Harry Maslin: melodica, synthesiser, vibraphone
Producers: David Bowie, Harry Maslin
Running time: 37:54
Studios: Cherokee and Record Plant, Los Angeles
Release date: 23 January 1976
Label: RCA Victor CPL1-1327 (UK), APL1-1327 (US)
Chart position: UK: 5, US: 3

'I'm in a very lucky position of not wanting to fly, so I take a ship or a train or something', Bowie said in an interview on *The Dick Cavett Show* shortly after the release of *Young Americans*. The journey that may have informed *Station To Station* was most likely his epic Trans-Siberian express trip from Vladivostok on the sea of Japan to Moscow, taken with his childhood friend and collaborator Geoff McCormack in 1973. In early spring, the view from the train was an endless barren landscape of frosty fields and frozen ponds: 'It was like a glimpse into another age, another world, and it made a very strong impression on me'. That journey was one of a number of likely inspirations for the character The Thin White Duke – a chilly figure struck by stark white lights onstage in an attempt to capture the mood of Berlin cabaret. Bowie's new persona was not a pleasant fellow, and his theme song 'Station To Station' describes him as 'Throwing darts in lovers' eyes'.

'David had gone levels into insanity', commented Earl Slick. The insanity wasn't just drug-induced, however, for David had sunk to awful depths of insecurity and paranoia in his now isolated existence in suburban Los Angeles. He'd begun storing his urine in the fridge, afraid of witches using it to cast spells on him, convinced that esoteric forces were trying to manipulate him – he was, in truth, becoming delusional. No wonder his fevered cocaine-enhanced imagination conjured up The Thin White Duke.

Three months after the release of *Station To Station* in April 1976, Bowie was detained by customs officials on the Russian/Polish border after they discovered a cache of Nazi memorabilia in his luggage. Bowie later said he'd lost his memory of the whole era and could not remember any of the album sessions or anything else from his miserable time in L.A.

The cover shot is the first of two album covers with an image from director Nic Roeg's 1976 UK art-house movie *The Man Who Fell To Earth*, where Bowie plays a disguised alien trying to save his home planet from an ecological disaster. His character, Thomas Newton, was to re-emerge in the 2022 TV sequel, where actor Bill Nighy played the character as an older alien exile.

'Station To Station' (Bowie)
Producer Harry Maslin may have felt out of his depth, having only been brought in initially to produce two tracks on *Young Americans*. The young engineer now had the more difficult job of divining Bowie's wishes at the Record Plant as he put his new band through their paces on partial songs mostly created in the studio and on the hoof. But Bowie's instincts invariably came through as he shouted instructions for Earl Slick to produce a feedback wail that masqueraded as the grinding, squealing wheels of a train pulling out of the station. The result as the train pans from speaker to speaker is wonderfully evocative. There are also two lovely guitar arpeggios from Carlos Alomar that perfectly complement the more-eruptive sounds. The whole band then kicks into a motoric groove. (Bowie had been listening to Krautrock bands like Neu! and Kraftwerk.)

Though Bowie was now an amnesiac with drug psychosis, the title track is a musical masterwork painted with thick, gorgeous oils on a massive canvas. Strokes of magical Mussorgsky guitar are applied by Earl Slick and Carlos Alomar, with effects that open the album, making it seem as if you are embarking on a strange train journey, complete with creaking wheels and chugging mechanical gears. Chopin-like piano parts ripple across the sound landscapes, played by Bruce Springsteen's E Street Band keyboard maestro Roy Bittan. And topping it all off is that exact and unforgiving rhythm section of Dennis Davis and George Murray.

'The return of the thin white duke', Bowie intones as he introduces his unfriendly character who is back from some wilderness and is 'bending sounds' ... 'lost in my circles'. The regurgitated rhythm churns onward as he continues to bemoan his lot, mentioning a 'magical movement from Kether to Malkuth'. This is a reference to the Jewish *Kabbalah* and he's not alone in becoming obsessed with such works (the *Kabbalah* and other mystic tomes are meat and drink to many scholars and theologists) – in music, though, not so much. Bowie had always enjoyed delving into such works, having mentioned esoterists such as Aleister Crowley and Friedrich Nietzsche in earlier songs.

The song shifts gear about halfway through, moving into a more uplifting and inspirational 2nd movement with majestic piano motifs from Roy Bittan. But here, the lyric refers entirely to a romanticised past: 'Once there were sunbirds to soar with and once I could never be down'. These memories of a happier time in the past contrast with the earlier turgid thoughts on the train in the first part of the song, for the movement from Kether to Malkuth is, unfortunately, one from the higher states of mind to the lower. He is pictured studying a diagram of Kabbalistic lore on the rear cover of the 1992 Rykodisc CD reissue.

The song surges ahead with Bowie crying, 'It's too late, the European canon is here'. There is real fear in his voice, as if he's being carried away on a tide.

'Golden Years' (Bowie)

Heavy reverb is used on this memorable guitar riff and the strange percussive handclaps and finger snaps that occasionally sound like cracking bones, all giving the song a dreamy decadence. Mirrored by delicate melodica, Bowie's vocal is couched in a miasma of sound that's full of nuance and backed with doo-wop backing vocals.

This is the song that most of all evokes the character of the Gouster, a term that had been considered as the title for the previous album, a character who dressed in an obscure, hip street fashion of 60s black culture that really appealed to Bowie, as the song is all about attitude and cool, as displayed on the single's picture cover: Bowie looking smart, with an insouciant cigarette dangling from his lips. The lyrics suggest a fine, luxurious trip 'in the back of a dream car 20 foot long', David singing of taking his lover back to their old haunts in the less salubrious areas of town just to show off his success and ostentatious wealth.

But there is an undertow of strangeness and uncertainty to the track as if all this is just a star trip, that the golden years themselves are really a materialist illusion, that really fame itself is a trap: 'Doing alright but gotta get smart'. The song ends with advice which echoes that given at the end of the *Diamond Dogs* album: 'Run for the shadows'.

'Word On A Wing' (Bowie)

This plea to God for patience and intercession is the album's most remarkable track. Bowie had toyed with gospel music on *Young Americans* – especially on the outtake 'Who Can I Be Now?', but this is actual prayer in song: 'Sweet name I'm born once again/Lord, I kneel and offer you this word on a wing'.

In 1980, Bowie commented, 'It was the first time I'd really seriously thought about Christ and God in any depth, and 'Word On A Wing' was a protection'. Interestingly, he went on to say that the crisis that brought on this need for spiritual protection was exacerbated by pressures associated with being on set for the production of his first feature film. He started filming *The Man Who Fell To Earth* three months before the album sessions began, filming in Arizona and White Sands, New Mexico, quite near places where UFOs were often spotted and where the infamous Roswell incident occurred. Bowie was intimidated by the requirements of being on a movie set, having no previous experience. He was also in free fall due to his drug habits: '...a good exhibition of somebody literally falling apart in front of you ... I was stoned out of my mind from beginning to end'. All of this is evident in the song, with a powerful and moving vocal performance given a bravura backing by the band and judicious backing vocals. At times, it almost sounds as if David is crying: 'Lord, Lord, my breath lies like a word on a wing'.

91

'TVC 15' (Bowie)

This futuristic fable is the album's most fun track and, of course, was a minor hit single following the success of 'Golden Years'. Apparently inspired by Iggy Pop's girlfriend's obsession with television, it's a quirky love song to the small screen, with David's tongue firmly in his cheek. Bowie's new obsession, he assures us, is his 'main feature', alerting us to the fact that his TV is actually the object of his passion in this song.

The track has features of the early rock 'n' roll style popularised by Little Richard and Jerry Lee Lewis, with stride piano at the beginning but great backup from the two guitarists Slick and Alomar – one playing long overdriven bent notes whilst the other plays dampened arpeggios. The whole arrangement is precise and full of tricks and quirks that are in-keeping with the light-hearted subject matter. Bowie even plays some tight little sax runs as if we're back in the glam rock era for a moment. But the song still has a subtle edge to it – something nagging at the back of your mind about how TV and technology are taking over our lives surreptitiously.

'Stay' (Bowie)

'Stay' is about the inevitable tension between two people attracted to each other who are not yet sure about it. The sound is thick and syrupy with a mesh of guitar sounds. The guitarists really stretch out over a funk rhythm in a display of very tight group playing. It didn't seem to have the same precise structure when played live, where it was morphed into a more amorphic glut of sound. A live version was included on the 1993 Rykodisc reissue, and a complete concert live *In Nassau Coliseum '76* was included in the 2016 *Who Can I Be Now?* box set.

The sound of the two guitarists sparring over some extended musical sections is one of the most memorable things on *Station To Station*. Somehow, the strange swampy sound seems to draw you in, as if you're slowly slipping into the quicksand, very much like the effect alcohol and cocaine might've had on two people attracted to each other but uncertain. There's a certain magic about the situation and the music itself, Bowie's voice cajoling and inviting: 'Stay/That's what I meant to say/Or do something'.

'Wild Is The Wind' (Tiomkin)

Made famous by singer Johnny Mathis in 1957, this may seem a strange choice for Bowie, yet it's a bravura vocal performance and a fitting end to the album. Nina Simone – firebrand and doyen of the jazz scene – released a live version in 1966, which caught David's ear, 'her version really affected me', he commented in 1993. It's also true that he was toying with another Springsteen cover, perhaps inspired by E Street Band pianist Roy Bittan being in the band. Bowie's version of 'It's Hard To Be A Saint In The City' was released on *Best Of David Bowie 1969/1974*, along with other rarities. It sounds like a closing track, too, with a very powerful string arrangement and a sonorous delivery very much in keeping with the album's overall feel and heavy atmosphere, though, according to Bob Spitz in his 2009 book *Bowie: A Biography*, it was fellow artist and crooner Frank Sinatra's complementary comments, when he visited the album sessions, which led to it being used as the closer.

What makes 'Wild Is The Wind' the perfect closer is its sidestepping of the more edgy elements of Bowie's own songs with its romanticism from an older era, and it allows a long sigh of relief as the listener releases tension. It's a fine arrangement, with a spare piano and rhythm section interlaced with a lovely flanged guitar. Bowie has become ambitious here, and in his vocal technique, he uses every nuance of tone. He stills his breath as he enunciates each syllable of the line 'Don't you know?/You're life itself'.

Outtake
'It's Hard To Be A Saint In The City' (Springsteen)
This track has a prominent string arrangement and was certainly an attempt to produce a closing track for the album. It would've worked just as well as 'Wild Is The Wind' – in fact, the Springsteen song fits even better with the mood of the album. However, Bowie cannot have been happy with it, and indeed, he seems to have fluffed the vocal on the chorus at the end, singing much of it in falsetto when the earlier chorus had less falsetto and was more controlled – though this could easily have been solved by dropping-in the earlier vocal part as a replacement for the last chorus. Either way, it's a masterful reworking of the song from Springsteen's first album, and it gave Roy Bittan of the E Street Band a chance to sparkle on a song he didn't play on for the Bruce version where it was played by David Sancious.

This track can be found in the *Sound And Vision* box set and on *Best Of David Bowie 1969/1974.*

Low (1977)

David Bowie: vocals, backing vocals, guitar, bass, vibraphone, xylophone, synthesiser, harmonica, saxophone
Brian Eno: synthesiser, piano, backing vocals, guitar treatments
Roy Young: piano, Farfisa organ
Ricky Gardiner, Carlos Alomar: rhythm guitar, lead guitar
George Murray: bass
Dennis Davis: drums
Iggy Pop, Mary Hopkins: backing vocals
Eduard Meyer: cello
Peter Robinson, Paul Buckmaster: piano and synthesiser
Producers: David Bowie, Tony Visconti
Running time: 38:26
Studios: Chateau d'Herouville, France; Hansa, Berlin
Release date: 14 January 1977
Label: RCA Victor PL 12030 (UK), CPL1-2030 (US)
Chart position: UK: 2, US: 11

Low is an absolute watershed in Bowie's career. Having had his fill of The Thin White Duke and the craziness of his life in L.A., he now turned to his friend and early mentor Tony Visconti to find a different sound and move away from that tense and dissolute lifestyle. So they holed up in the Chateau d'Herouville again (where *Pin Ups* was recorded) and decided to produce a schizophrenic new music; one initial title for the album being *New Music: Night And Day*.

The memorable orange cover art is again a picture of David as the character from *The Man Who Fell To Earth*: the alien/human hybrid Thomas Jerome Newton. He is shown in profile: hence the joke often made about a 'low profile'. But this image references two distinct ideas. One is that Bowie so identified with the alien in the movie that he wanted his music to be closely associated with it. The other is that he was utterly alienated by the time the album was released, in retreat from his drug-addled life in L.A. and wanted to keep a low profile. He was looking for an escape to a simpler life.

He absconded to Berlin with Iggy Pop for the mixing of *Low*, taking a rather plain first-floor flat above a cycle shop at Hauptstrasse 155 in the Schoneberg district. Bowie has said that he began work on the album with friend and maverick ambient musician Brian Eno at the 'honky chateau' in France, with the beginnings of musical ideas that eventually became the first single *Sound And Vision*:

> That was the ultimate retreat song, the first thing I wrote with Brian in mind when we were working together at the Chateau. It was just the idea of getting out of America ... It was wanting to be put in a little cold room with omnipotent blue on the walls and blinds on the windows.

The music was inspired at least as much by work he'd done with arranger/ conductor Paul Buckmaster on the soundtrack for *The Man Who Fell To Earth* that was not produced in time to be used for the film. They'd recorded demos meant to convey something of the otherworldliness of the film: a science-fiction evocation of the alien character's home world. This really got David's creativity flowing as he considered who would be best to hone these ideas into something really astonishing. Side two of the album would be just such a surprising musical *tour de force* with Eno's help, though the record company didn't like it, this being the first occasion when a representative of RCA pleaded and begged David to produce instead 'another *Young Americans*'.

'Speed Of Life' (Bowie)
The opening track begins with treated synthesiser sounds that give the impression of a transformer powering down, instantly putting us in the Krautrock arena. We are then introduced to that imperious drum sound produced with the help of Visconti's oft-mythologised use of the Eventide Harmoniser, which intrigued David, as he was told its principle function was to 'fuck with the fabric of time'. And it did!

The first of two short instrumentals bookending side one of the original album, 'Speed Of Life' is extremely robotic and powers ahead mechanistically, with guitars playing a repeated phrase and the keyboards, with their dying transformer, butting in at the end of each bar until a short stasis is reached when the song slows momentarily as if waiting for the next mechanical cycle to begin.

'Breaking Glass' (Bowie, Davis, Murray)
Many of the songs simply began as studio jams, little musical ideas that were fleshed out with a few choice words once inspiration struck. This one credits bassist George Murray and drummer Dennis Davis with compositional input, with much time-fabric experimentation going on during the interludes before the words come in: angular music that is spiky and insistent.

The words describe the destruction of someone's room and the singer's supposed shame at what he has perpetrated: 'Don't look at the carpet/I drew something awful on it'. It's the song of someone struggling with demons, someone afraid of themselves and the crazed behaviour they exhibit. It doesn't offer any explanation, just 'You're a wonderful person/But you've got problems'.

It's worth pointing out that for an album so often lauded as synthesiser-based, all of the songs on side one are really guitar rock with funk rhythmic elements. Synths interject pointedly throughout, like the clarion call of the new technological world.

'What In The World' (Bowie)
'What in the world can I do?', David sings resignedly in the chorus of another song with a subtext of dangerous behaviour. 'What are you gonna do to the

95

real me?'. The singer exhibits an identity crisis, a need for love and a great deal of confusion.

The sound is more frantic. Intricate synth sounds are laced with harsh guitars again running wild, giving that sense of anxiety and disturbance. It's a giddy trip, addressed to a 'girl with grey eyes' who it seems is as uncertain as the narrator: 'Who are you gonna be to the real me?'. Who is the 'real me' in the song? David is *persona non grata*.

'Sound And Vision' (Bowie)

This shimmering diamond is the central feature of side one. It's a perfect piece of pop and so exactly honed that it was always difficult to replicate live as the arrangement of the song is so complex – there's a rhythm guitar with a tremolo effect against another rhythm, choppy and funky, allied to a Davis/ Murray bass/drums pattern front and centre. Then, rather than simply leading into the lead vocal, we first get a lovely backing vocal from Visconti's wife Mary Hopkins and a priceless little saxophone soupçon from David before his hesitant but soulful voice appears.

The song posits isolation as a restful and meditative place, with reminders that the things we take for granted – like television and music itself – are actually intrusions on the pristine silence, which is sometimes more valuable. Though the protagonist states he's 'Waiting for the gift of sound and vision', he seems to be in a blissed-out state, 'Drifting into my solitude/Over my head'.

The single was a great surprise to the record company, who'd insisted the album was unacceptable with its second side of otherworldly instrumentals. But the single was a big hit in several territories. This meant it would be easier to sell a follow-up with a similar MO. This was more than David could've hoped for, as he'd really put his neck on the line by championing his experimental instrumental tracks, and he must've felt totally validated by the success of this single and the album itself, especially in the UK, where weird was often seen as a positive in the music world. Another unforeseen plus about this song is that, at a time when punk rock was shaking things up in the music business, Bowie too was seen to be changing and was not left behind.

'Always Crashing In The Same Car' (Bowie)

This song has the eerie atmosphere of a dream but was absolutely inspired by a real event: David driving 'round and round the hotel car park' in a state of anxiety. This is symbolic of every strange *deja vu*-like occurrence in life and of every situation in which we feel trapped repeating the same mistakes. It's the perfect metaphor for David's life in L.A., from which he has just escaped – firstly to the recording studio in France and later to Berlin, where a new phase of his career was to begin in earnest.

The track has sublime lead guitar from Scottish musician Ricky Gardiner, formerly of prog rock band Beggars Opera. He plays on most of side one, but his elegiac guitar solo at the end of this track was a 'cosmic solo' according to *Guardian* journalist Ben Beaumont-Thomas in Gardiner's obituary. Visconti referred to Gardiner as a 'guitar genius' in the same piece, and we can be thankful that he was recruited, as he played an important role in kick-starting this fantastic phase of Bowie's oeuvre.

'Be My Wife' (Bowie)

The sole recipient of Bowie's strained cockney vocal style on the album, 'Be My Wife' comes across as a cranky throwback to the previous era's David, recalling the keyboard-heavy drama of 'Time' from *Aladdin Sane* and coming complete with a barrelhouse piano-part that throws the whole album off-kilter. Released as a single to follow up 'Sound And Vision', it is a strange bedfellow indeed. No explanation for the song's existence has come from Bowie, but he sometimes included it in live sets, announcing it as 'one of my favourites'. One way of looking at it is to see it as a disavowal of his marriage to Angie Bowie, which was shortly to come to a sticky end and a quirky way of saying that his true love was yet to be found.

'A New Career In A New Town' (Bowie)

A drum fill leads to spaced-out keyboards that seem to float on air, the bass drum keeping a simple heartbeat. It's the second instrumental and concludes side one in an otherworldly fashion. When the guitars and rhythm section kick in, it's with a wild jolt of energy, denoting David's fortitude in restarting his career when other musicians might've disappeared into the black hole of stardom in L.A.

Many years later, on Bowie's last tour following his 2003 *Reality* album, every concert began with the band arriving onstage to an instrumental eerily similar to this track – the central feature of which was Bowie's harmonica-playing. Even though his 'new career' would be as a Motorik-inspired synthesiser instrumentalist and explorer of new and avant-garde musical ideas, he was still reminding us of his roots in R&B, blues and Dylan-esque psych rock.

'Warszawa' (Bowie, Eno)

The alien symphony that comprises side two is one of the most arresting surprises you get in rock music. It is so remarkable and unique that it leaves one wondering how such an extreme change in musical style came about. No doubt it was, to some extent, in response to the horrible times Bowie endured in Los Angeles, with his concomitant need to curb his drug habit and his need to make a clean break, forsaking anything that reminded him of that time. Yet all the elements were in place to produce it, the main one being that Bowie was tentatively tasked with creating soundtrack music for his first feature film.

It's easy to forget that his first love was saxophone, so jazz had played a large part in his early musical education, his brother Terry introducing him to saxophonist John Coltrane and trumpet player Miles Davis. Despite the saxophone being only deployed fitfully on this track and side two's closing piece 'Subterraneans', the jazz feel was noted by Donny McCaslin (who played on Bowie's last album *Blackstar*) and Dylan Howe, who have both covered music from *Low* in the jazz idiom. The third thing it's important to bear in mind is that Bowie was always interested in the *idea* of extra-terrestrial life and UFOs (one of his later songs was called 'Born In A UFO').

'Warszawa' – the opening movement of David's alien symphony (later there would actually be 'Symphony No. 1 (*Low*)' when composer Philip Glass used parts of the *Low* and *"Heroes"* albums as the basis for the symphony) – begins subtle and gloomy, and at first only a simple dolorous note ploddingly plays like a faint heartbeat. This is followed by a more strident theme played on synths, accompanied by wordless voices, which is really only an introduction to the first sung section where Bowie introduces his new alien language of which a few words do seem to equate with known English words. 'Malio' sounds like the word for illness in many romantic languages, such as the English word 'malady' (adopted from the French 'Malade'). A sick, dying planet?

This piece must've surely also been inspired by that long Trans-Siberian train journey undertaken back in 1973, which gave Bowie a long uninterrupted vista of a bleak wintery landscape, arriving in Warsaw (Warszawa) *en route* to Paris after a stop off in Moscow. He again visited Warsaw with Iggy Pop in 1976 and obviously had been much affected by its still-visible post-war decay, Bowie commenting that it caught 'the very bleak atmosphere I got from the city'. On one of these trips, it's known that Bowie bought a record by the Śląsk Polish National Song and Dance Ensemble. This sound of Polish voices influenced his invented language, though seemingly otherworldly, inspiring this strange melange of atonal vocalisations.

'Art Decade' (Bowie)

The second movement of Bowie's alien symphony maintains the moody atmosphere but is a little faster. It's still very measured and majestic, with several futuristic noises, creaks and groans like gigantic doors opening and closing and bubbling sounds like liquids moving through giant pipes. Unlike Eno's ambient music, it has a clear melody underpinned by a Chamberlin rhythm that keeps the piece moving relentlessly to its conclusion.

When Bowie conceived of these pieces of music, he may have used the ideas in Walter Tevis' novel *The Man Who Fell To Earth* as his scene templates. There is excitement in this music, even though the themes of a doomed world and an ancient technological civilisation struggling to survive are depressing. The synths move inexorably onwards, seemingly depicting massive cities and machinery that have hopes to send out spaceships to find help for their planet.

'Weeping Wall' (Bowie)

The third movement is the alien scherzo, with more of an upbeat rhythm. The grief denoted by the title references the ancient wall in Jerusalem, where adherents of the Jewish faith go to mourn the destruction of the temple. The track indeed features mournful choir-like vocals. Is it meant to represent the denizens of Thomas Jerome Newton's alien home world coming to an end?

Next is a section of treated guitar/keyboard that holds a stronger melody for a while before the track descends into a morass of howling voices and strafing electronic noises. This track (and, in fact, many of the synthetic sounds on side two) strangely recalls incidental sounds in episodes of the original TV show *Star Trek*, though this may be simply because that was also one of the first shows with sounds evoking other worlds and futuristic technology. In fact, that was a feature of much music created in the 1980s, too, when synths and programmed rhythms became the norm and music took on all the trappings of the emerging new technology. *Low* was at the vanguard for synthpop and new synthetic sounds.

'Subterraneans' (Bowie)

The concluding chapter of *Low* is the most unforgiving. It's not only a strange and otherworldly piece, but it creeps up on you in a strange minor-key advance of shifting synths for the first three minutes – as if being tuned in from some lost space between stations on the dial – before there comes a thin wail of saxophone. Ethereal voices soon enter – mostly Bowie's – in a resigned chorus of wordless moans. It gives a sense of chaos swirling around with an incipient feeling, the searching sax still sending out small tendrils of tone.

Eventually, the track comes to a second section, where David's lone voice soars above the circling backing voices, and he's singing in an alien language again. David was not alone in this eccentric way of creating lyrics, though. Later, Icelandic band Sigur Ros found inspiration for singing in an imaginary language, citing the need to find something that fitted the mood of the music better than existing words. Also, in Rodney Bingenheimer's downtown Los Angeles English disco of the glam-rock era, there was a house band called Zolar X who sang in their own invented alien speech. They *must've* been on Bowie's radar.

What of the words sung here? 'Failing star' seems to imply a dying star or a supernova rather than a planet. 'Care line' seems compassionate, as if those who cared had created a line to be used to pull the suffering citizens of the failing star to safety. But in the end, this is a piece of music that also expresses wonder, perhaps because the other likely inspiration for the piece was Jack Kerouac's beat treatise of the same title – a novella depicting the beginnings of a forbidden romance in the underground bars and jazz dives of late-1950s San Francisco, with all the excitement of a new subcultural movement frowned upon by staid society. The repeated refrain, which sounds like 'Shirley, Shirley, Shirley-own', is more akin to something from 1950s jazz being sung in some shadowy underground bar. The alien symphony plays out in just such a modern jazz style, with the sax blowing free-form as the shady chords continue shifting and churning on.

Another interesting, inspirational idea for this track came from the book *The Coming Race* – an early science-fiction novel Bowie mentioned on the *Hunky Dory* album in the song 'Oh! You Pretty Things'. The novel's author, Edward Bulwer-Lytton, wrote of a subterranean race in a shadowy underworld who were described as strange and beautiful creatures that closely resembled angels. Their power source, known as Vril, was something sought by the Nazi Party's Thule society – a group of officers who specialised in myth and occult secrets and believed in such an underground realm as something real. And we already know that David was fascinated by the Nazis' search for occult powers.

Outtakes/Demos
'Some Are' (Bowie, Eno)
This first appeared on the 1991 Rykodisc reissue and later on the instrumental compilation album *All Saints*. It has the same chilly synthesiser mood as side two of *Low* but also has lyrics: 'Sleigh bells in snow/cinder colour blazing eyes/some are bound to fail'. The track gives the impression of a sad episode from a war, with retreating soldiers marching solemnly through the snowy wilderness, Bowie himself suggesting, 'Images of the failed Napoleonic force stumbling back through Smolensk ... A *Weltschmerz* indeed'. (Bowie is here using a German term for 'world-weariness' from the world of art and literature).

'All Saints' (Bowie, Eno)
Sounding like a dry run for the other synthesiser instrumentals on this album, this rather harsh-sounding piece possibly has more Eno in it than Bowie, lacking the latter's more melodic, structured touch. Similar to some of Eno's work on *Another Green World*, it was later the title track of the above-mentioned compilation, which was originally Bowie's privately made collection for friends but given a wider release in 1993.

"Heroes" (1977)

Personnel:
David Bowie: vocals, backing vocals, guitar, keyboards, koto, saxophone
Robert Fripp: lead guitar
Brian Eno: synthesisers, keyboards, treatments
Carlos Alomar: rhythm guitar
George Murray: bass
Davis Davis: drums, percussion
Tony Visconti: percussion, backing vocals
Antonia Maass: backing vocals
Producers: Tony Visconti, David Bowie
Running time: 40:19
Studio: Hansa studio 2, Berlin
Release date: 14 October 1977
Label: RCA Victor PL 12522 (UK), RCA Victor AFL1-2522 (US)
Chart position: UK: 3, US: 35

Based in Berlin, Bowie was now industriously producing songs at Hansa
Studios by the Berlin wall, for both himself and Iggy Pop – whose albums
from this era (*The Idiot* and *Lust For Life*) are as much a part of Bowie's then
vogue for musical reinvention as were his own.

Bowie was immersed in the new culture of Krautrock: Amon Duul 2,
Kraftwerk and Neu!. He and Iggy's nights included exotic experiences at
the arty nightclub Chez Romy Haag with its black décor, which was run by
David's transgender friend and confidant Romy Haag, who referred to it as
'a disco with Art Deco furniture and cocktails'. Going through strictures with
his estranged wife Angie – who sometimes appeared unexpectedly, trying
to reignite their marriage – David was also unhappy with failing to extricate
himself fully from his old Mainman management contract with Tony Defries,
as the agreement was to secure Defries income from anything David recorded
up to 1981.

There was, however, a huge sense of relief due to his new low-key lifestyle
(not wanting to be recognised, Bowie had a very plain haircut and sported
a flat cap). He later wrote about his life at this time on the song 'Where Are
We Now?' from his penultimate masterpiece *The Next Day*. He obviously felt a
great fondness for this time in Berlin, which had given him a chance to take
stock, change direction and get more control of his life.

He also relied a lot on his personal aide Coco Schwab, who had entered
David's service on the 1974 tour. Not known for his culinary skills, it's likely
that Schwab made every meal for him when he chose to eat at his and Iggy's
prosaic flat. In fact, during the *Low* sessions, Brian Eno said he'd seen a
hungry Bowie simply sit down and crack two raw eggs into his mouth.

If *Low* was the beginning of a rehabilitation phase after the lows of his
L.A. existence, *"Heroes"* was a kind of recognition of just how dangerous

his life had become, with some of the songs referencing dangerous feelings, stress, despair and suffering of an acute type. If anything was helping Bowie overcome these feelings, it was a slow turning outward, an ability to focus on the plight of others, and tracks like 'Neukoln' (a sax-centred piece on another largely instrumental second side), which evoked the struggles of life in the poorer quarters of Berlin – especially Neukoln itself, a multicultural urban area with a high level of immigration from North Africa.

The album cover – like that of Iggy's *The Idiot* – depicts Bowie in a pose copied from the painting Roquairol by German expressionist Erich Heckel. This curiously angular pose represents the music on both albums very well. The two albums are not easy to listen to: they are spiky and scary, even a bit disturbed.

'Beauty And The Beast' (Bowie)

Like entering the steaming jungle, this song is certainly more beast than beauty and begins the album with a strong rock sensibility, odd sound effects impinging on the mounting tribal drum rhythm, as Robert Fripp's guitar enters the fray with gusto. Bowie's treated voice is edgy and describes a life 'gone wrong', where he calls for a priest and generally decries life in the urban malaise of the city. Fripp's guitar weaves in and out of a heavily treated thundering keyboard riff that sounds like the beast of the title lumbering past, jaws slavering.

There is a strained, extraordinary angst in the vocal. 'I wanted to believe me'. Bowie is at once denouncing his former self (He can't even remember the *Station To Station* sessions) and castigating the notoriety of his existence as a rock star: an ambivalent sexuality cheapened by fame. Any chance encounter with beauty might inevitably bring out the beast in our personality. The song implies that no one is exempt from these feelings: 'You can't say no to the beauty and the beast'.

'Joe The Lion' (Bowie)

Bowie demonstrated an array of vocal techniques on the album, and one of them is a hysterical and rather deranged vocal tone. From the moment you hear it, you can't help but be aware that it's sung from the point of view of someone in some sort of pain. The music is quite understated for this one, as if beneath the exterior anxiety of the lead vocal is depression or a flatness of affect. Guitars burst through from time to time, and there's a restrained lead line from Fripp, but the song has the type of restricted melody that is more exclaimed than sung. The lyric begins like a joke told in a pub: 'Joe the lion walks into a bar...'

American performance artist Chris Burden obviously shook David to the core with a piece called 'Trans-Fixed', which Burden and his attorney performed in 1974 at a speedway, where the artist allowed himself to be *crucified* on the rear of a Volkswagen Beetle. For Bowie, this Christ of the auto-age was an oracle and could give you a reading like a mystic: 'Nail me to my car and I'll tell you who you are'. This is juxtaposed against a surreal and funny take on the modern nine-to-five life of the city dweller: 'It's Monday/ You slither down the greasy pipe/So far so good'.

A recurring theme on the album (seen also in 'Sons Of The Silent Age' and 'Blackout') is the idea that something about modern life is not quite right.

"Heroes" (Bowie, Eno)

A lovely elegiac song with two definite vocal styles, "Heroes" owes the speech marks in the title to the idea of 'ironic distance'. These are 'heroes', but not the kind in comic books or Greek mythology – these are everyday people who make their lives better by dreaming of a better life and simply living life to the full. In the beginning, Bowie sings in his deeper, richer ballad style. But when he later repeats the first verse, it's with the anxiety-inducing and more vulnerable style full of unrestrained emotions that he'd recently honed to perfection.

The story is that from the window of the recording studio, which overlooked the looming Berlin wall with its mounted gun-placements and guards, Bowie glimpsed a couple meeting in secret for a snog. (He was not aware until later that it was actually producer Tony Visconti and backing vocalist Antonia Maass.) The scene filled Bowie with elation, and he thought of all the things ordinary people do (or dream of doing) that, for a moment, can lift them out of even the most depressing scenario. (Nothing could be more a symbol of this than lovers kissing under a massive edifice built in the name of political and military intransigence.) The image recalls the *1984* character Winston Smith, his illicit love Julia, and Bowie's new relationship with Romy Haag in Berlin, which brought him such solace in a time of great upheaval in his life.

Eventually, this song was recognised as one of Bowie's greatest achievements, and it's now hailed as a masterpiece of rock music, with Jason Draper of *Dig!* magazine commenting that it has 'become embraced as a euphoric anthem for any grand occasion' – Bowie himself couldn't explain why this was and said he was 'not sure what that song means anymore, which is kind of exciting!'

The incredible multitracked guitar is a thing of beauty in itself. Visconti has said that he simply allowed Fripp to play a number of lines over the chord sequence, then simply melded them together into the morass of wailing, feedback-drenched guitar that curves gracefully through the track's sonic mélange. Some of the lead lines are so mercurial and flow so effortlessly from Fripp's fingers that they almost defy description: it is a truly beautiful sound. But at the time, the single was not a great success, only reaching 24 in the UK and not charting at all in the less-impressed US.

Bowie famously unveiled the song on the last episode of Marc Bolan's TV show *Marc*, just before Bolan was killed in a car crash. They also co-wrote the two songs 'Madman' and 'Standing Next To You' around this time (only murky rehearsal recordings exist), the second of which they played together at the end of the show, though Bolan was drunk and fell off the stage before Bowie began singing. They worked together on Bowie's early single 'The Prettiest Star' and on the album version of 'Memory Of A Free Festival', and Marc said that Bowie played on the T. Rex songs 'I Really Love You Babe' from *Bolan's Zip Gun* (probably harmonica), and 'Casual Agent' from the penultimate T. Rex album *Futuristic Dragon*. David cared for Marc so greatly that he made a special effort to play 'Heroes' on Marc's children's TV show at a time when Bolan was trying to rehabilitate himself and his career.

'Sons Of The Silent Age' (Bowie)
With an opening of transcendental saxophone from Bowie, this song is as schizophrenic as the two vocal styles in the previous song. The verses – slow and in a stately, rather depressed mood – describe an urban life of self-deception, showing the 'sons of the silent age' to be largely unemotional people trapped in the daily drudgery, who 'pace their rooms like a cell's dimensions'.

The B-section vocal morphs into a soulful pleading that seems to be from another Bowie era, with lyrics that sound like early rock 'n' roll – 'Baby, I won't ever let you go' – as if there's an escape from the tedium of life depicted in the verses, maybe with the advent of rock 'n' roll itself. The magic of rock 'n' roll awoke sleepers from their boring lives in the 1950s, and they need to change desperately, as the sons of the silent age seem pretty dejected: 'They rise for a year or two and make war/Search through their one-inch thoughts/Then decide it couldn't be done'.

'Blackout' (Bowie)
There is a palpable sense of despair in this track. Erupting from silence like some sort of sudden attack or fit, the music is feral and frightening. 'The weather's grim/There's ice on the cages' sings Bowie, and it appears we are back in the jungle of the opening track 'Beauty And The Beast', as 'Panthers are ... stalking, screaming'. But there's confusion in the lyric too – 'Someone's back in town/The chips are down' could be a reference to David's wife Angie turning up out of the blue as she was known to do, trying to entice him back into his old ways. Also, he's pleading with someone to 'stay tonight', or he will take a plane and fly away. There is no doubt that David felt this song very acutely and it reflected his own despair at both his failing marriage and the crazy L.A. lifestyle he was attempting to escape from. This was a time of change for David and he had certain fears – as ever – about his mental health: 'Get me to a doctor'.

Side one ends with this crazy exhortation to escape a situation in which he feels helpless and out of control. Not many songs reference illness and alienation quite so viscerally; there's a constant chorus line of 'Get me off the streets'. The backing vocals simply mirror the madness: 'Get some protection' and especially with regard to his music 'Get some direction'.

'V2 Schneider' (Bowie)
Suddenly, it's as if Bowie is back in the King Bees in 1964. He has again produced a sonic surprise with this saxophone-centred, mostly instrumental track that harks back to the early rock 'n' roll era. Again, it's beneficial to remember that David's first love was the saxophone, in particular, its use on the early Little Richard singles.

Yet, schizophrenically, the V2 in the title is a reference to the German missile used during World War II, so perhaps it should be no surprise that the music harks back to the post-war era already noted in 'Sons Of The Silent Age'. One section of the song suddenly seems steeped in 1950s rock 'n' roll.

The Schneider of the title (the title is the track's only sung part) is a likely reference to German musician Florian Schneider, founder member of Kraftwerk.

'Sense Of Doubt' (Bowie)
A sense of deep gloom now pervades. As ever with these instrumentals, there is the influence of Eno to take into account; there's more than a suggestion of his fingerprints on this one. I've heard it used as incidental music for a news report about maritime pollution, and it has the repetitive three-note keyboard riff that indicates a feeling of depression and dissociation, interspersed with various discordant sound effects and ethereal ARP synthesiser.

'Moss Garden' (Bowie, Eno)
So Japanese that it could be used as soundtrack music to any Miyazaki film, Bowie here distinguished himself as a player of the Japanese instrument the koto, which has a sound similar to a harp. It is so beautiful and delicate; it's trilling almost the sound of another plane of reality. This is one of David's most sublime instrumentals, with Brian Eno providing a floating keyboard bed from which Bowie's melodic playing rises like wind chimes.

'Neukoln' (Bowie, Eno)
We are plunged again into despair in this uncompromising aural portrait of an area Bowie frequented in Berlin at the time. His impressive saxophone playing elevates this track beyond the usual; its cadences rise from an aural bazar-basket, like a rearing snake of sound. The Turkish/North African section of Berlin, Neukoln, has always been a cosmopolitan but unsung region of the city.

'The Secret Life Of Arabia' (Bowie, Eno, Alomar)
A pointer to the music on the next album *Lodger*, this closing song takes us on a midnight camel ride to a desert oasis. A lot of the tracks on *Lodger* – a

105

travelogue of sorts – were to depict other cultures and countries. The song has strong rhythmic guitar from Alomar and a nice three-note keyboard riff that adds extra mystery. What is the secret that's referred to? It would surprise me if this wasn't the spiritual life to which Bowie aspired, as, with his interest in all things occult, he would've come across the mystics of Arabia, Sufism, Islam, the whirling dervishes and the syncretism of the Bahais.

Outtakes/Demos
'Abdulmajid' (Bowie)
Another track with a North African/Arabian soundscape, this is the last of Bowie's then-current crop of instrumentals and one with a curious aspect of predestination, for Abdulmajid was the surname of his future wife, the supermodel Iman. Bowie could *not* have known this, and yet here's proof that the name held significance for him long before he proposed to Iman on a boat on the Seine in 1992.

A haunting keyboard figure comes in to dignify a rather pedestrian percussion track. It must've made him smile all those years later that he'd seen his future wife's name in the crystal ball 15 years before they were together.

'Madman/Standing Next To You' (Bowie, Bolan)
Bolan and Bowie worked on these two songs during downtime for their respective albums. The songs are only known from bootleg copies of studio sessions/rehearsals where it's difficult to tell who is playing what. 'Madman' was eventually resurrected and released as a single by the 1980s band The Cuddly Toys. Though it got limited airplay, it was a decent glam-inspired tribute.

As already stated, the two men played the short intro of 'Standing Next To You' during the closing credits of the last episode of *Marc*. Bolan was drunk and fell off the stage, leaving David in fits of laughter. Unfortunately, it was the last he would see of his old friend and fellow London boy.

Lodger (1979)

Personnel:
David Bowie: vocals, backing vocals, guitar, keyboards
Adrian Belew: lead guitar, rhythm guitar, mandolin
Brian Eno: piano, keyboards, effects, backing vocals
Tony Visconti: guitar, mandolin
Carlos Alomar: guitar, drums, backing vocals
George Murray: bass
Dennis Davis: drums
Sean Meyes: piano
Simon House: mandolin, violin, backing vocals
Roger Powell: synthesiser
Stan Harrison: saxophone
Producers: David Bowie, Tony Visconti
Running time: 34:38
Studios: Mountain, Switzerland; Record Plant, New York
Release date: 25 May 1979
Label: RCA Victor BOW LP1 (UK), AQL1-3254 (US)
Chart position: UK: 4, US: 20

Recorded in Switzerland at an old Montreux casino with Adrian Belew performing his guitar theatrics on several key tracks, this album showed Bowie truly maturing into the multifaceted entertainer he was always bound to be. The record includes ballads, rock songs, strange discordant art rock, and all sorts of experimental songs. Belew – whom David discovered playing in a bar with Frank Zappa – was poached to play on Bowie's next tour, which led to the live *Stage* album issued the year before *Lodger*.

Experimentation was still the order of the day at the sessions, with Eno wheeling out his well-known 'oblique strategies' cards, which were meant to inspire musicians to try something different. As a result, sometimes the tracks were a bit hit-and-miss, with some of the strategies possibly getting in the way. But overall, it's a fascinating travelogue of Bowie's recent holidays in Africa and elsewhere, with a definite focus on culture and society.

The 2017 Tony Visconti remix included in the box set *A New Career In A New Town* attempted to improve on the rather thin original mix, giving the drums more crispness and presence and giving instruments in the soundstage more space, occasionally using slightly different original session tracks. As a whole, this mix is now truly definitive to me.

The cover is a homage to the self-portraits of Egon Schiele, whose art the Nazis considered to be subversive and burned in Berlin during the war. Shiele's art could seem raw and sometimes unforgiving, though the cover shot showed David as if he'd fallen from a great height and was squashed: an image he revisited in the 1993 song (about suicide), 'Jump They Say'. The image is weirdly presented as a postcard from the artist, in a similar style to Bruce Springsteen's first album *Greetings From Asbury Park*. It's a case of mixed metaphors here, though, as Bowie's idea of presenting a victim of suicide as something you'd want on a postcard is a little odd, to say the least. It's a postcard from the edge.

The important thing to note about the album is that Bowie felt he had more control of his life now, was looking healthier and was ready to take on the world, having identified one of his most important traits as a writer: he was interested in culture and social anthropology. His opportunities to travel the world not only provided travelogues similar to *Lodger* but also opened him up to the art of different cultures, their music and peoples: ideas that are central to an understanding of Bowie's work.

'Fantastic Voyage' (Bowie, Eno)

Dennis Davis' precise and measured drum fill starts the album – the opening salvo for a ballad that clearly shows Bowie's interest in world politics, US foreign policy and the need to back away from the arms race. 'They wipe out an entire race/But I've got to write it down so it won't be forgotten', he sings as the song moves forward in a stately way. It's a subtle and nuanced track that reveals a newer, more socially conscious Bowie observing his own culture first and foremost, aware that his much-loved America has lost its way. This didn't stop him from eventually making America his home, however.

'African Night Flight' (Bowie, Eno)

This is supposedly based on the 1957 Dale Hawkins rockabilly hit 'Suzie Q' played backwards. Bowie said in *Melody Maker* in 1979 that he and Eno simply reversed that chord sequence to create this oddity. With a tricky beat played on a cheese grater and the bass notes of a piano, this curate's egg of a track displays Bowie's newfound love of travel and, in particular, a visit to Africa shortly before the commencement of the *Lodger* sessions. Here, he tries hard to give the sound a rhythmic sense of danger, assisted by Brian Eno with his many instrumental treatments.

An African chant adds to the sense of place, although 'His burning eye will see me through' tends to suggest the narrator is appealing to tribal African gods. Many of the songs on *Lodger* use Bowie's role-playing skills as much as his musical ones.

'Move On' (Bowie)

Again, the rhythms dominate, sounding very similar to Buddy Holly's early rock 'n' roll single 'Peggy Sue'. Travelling is inevitably the theme, but this time in a general sense, as it was in many early blues songs such as 'Got To Travel On' and 'Gotta Move On': typical titles for the idiom. Bowie's version of this type of song morphs into a much more romantic section with the names of several countries he loves: 'Cyprus is my island' and 'Spent some nights in old Kyoto'. Again, there are backing vocals meant to evoke foreign tongues Bowie hopes will recreate his experiences of other cultures.

'Yassassin' (Bowie)

'Yassassin' is Turkish for 'Have a long life', and is certainly sung from the point of view of an immigrant in a foreign city – most likely Berlin as with 'Neukoln' on *"Heroes"*, and it depicts the dislocation amongst people who've found themselves at sea in the permissive-yet-discriminatory west: 'You want to fight, but I don't want to leave or drift away'. The song features a strange caterwauling violin from Simon House, but the reggae rhythm is somewhat misplaced. As a whole, it provides a genuine feeling of strangeness and alienation.

'Red Sails' (Bowie, Eno)

This song is an excellent example of Eno working with Bowie to produce exciting rock music. It has a new wave/punk ebullience about it, with an up-tempo pop thrust, the most fantastic mix of discordant lead guitar from Belew, as well as anxious, emotional vocals from Bowie in his guise as a simple Chinese peasant: 'Red sails/Thunder Ocean'. It's really such a great closer for side one of the original LP, and like many other tracks from the so-called Berlin Period, it was influential in the emerging new-romantic scene, inspiring bands such as Japan. Its spiky tone was also detectable in the sound of Wire and Bill Nelson's Red Noise.

'DJ' (Bowie)

This is Bowie's commentary on the cult of the DJ, sung from the point of view of the generic DJ who seems central to any understanding of the music scene of the 21st Century, although the song was written before DJs truly became pop stars themselves.

With Simon House's invasive violin and Adrian Belew's distinctive treated guitar all over it, it was a strange choice for a single and only made the lowly chart placing of 30 in the UK.

Bowie makes it clear through his hysterical and crazed vocal that this DJ is losing his mind due to the pressure on him to play the right tracks and to keep the records spinning. Bowie himself commented that 'if you have 30 seconds of silence, your career is over!' But with hindsight, one can say that it is also prophetic, detailing how the cult of personality dominates the idea of being a DJ, 'I am the DJ! I am what I say!' and heralding the 21st century with DJs given much more exalted status in musical culture.

'Look Back In Anger' (Bowie)

"You know who I am', he said', Bowie studiously intones as the song breaks in murderously. It has a fantastic rhythm guitar from Carlos Alomar and powerful, turbulent drumming from Dennis Davis. It moves at a frenetic pace.

It's a story about an angel who spends his time waiting for an unknown event, with crumpled wings and a cry of 'It's time we should be going'. Most commentators assume this is the angel of death, but I'm not so sure, as the angel seems a little too human for that since he 'leafed through a magazine' and seems likely to be a guardian angel. It actually ties in with early songs like 'The Supermen'.

Bowie's idea is that the angel is tired of humanity going through its materialist motions and longs for us to accept our spiritual destiny as divine humans who care for themselves and the planet better. This makes sense of the title, which harks back to the 1950s angry-young-men movement in the UK (a parallel in some ways to the Beat Generation in the US) and to John Osborn's book *Look Back In Anger* about a disaffected young man who is angry at society.

This track was given an extended remix in 1988 (included on the 1991 Rykodisc CD) because Bowie was working with the dancers La La La Human Steps, and this song lent itself well to a dramatic dance routine.

'Boys Keep Swinging' (Bowie)
This cryptic and rather sarcastic take on growing up as a boy in the late 20th century has its teeth firmly sunk into Western culture's more feminist take on existence. None of the things listed in the song – such as 'Life is a pop of the cherry' – are true, though they might've been said about masculine existence in the early 1960s when he began his career. The video hammered the point home, showing Bowie in drag, not always in the most flattering way, smearing his makeup and generally seeming pretty disenchanted. Some of the musicians played instruments they were unfamiliar with (perhaps at Eno's suggestion), and this makes the song sound quirky and unique, if a little disjointed, though it's certainly Belew playing his most outrageous guitar solo ever.

'Repetition' (Bowie)
This dull and flat track mirrors its horrific subject matter: domestic abuse. Bowie later tackled the subject matter in a more oblique, melodic way with the song 'Too Dizzy' (with intentional black humour) on the 1987 album *Never Let Me Down* (later deleted from his catalogue). With the approach of almost slogging through it, possibly at the suggestion of one of Eno's hilarious 'oblique strategies' card suggestions, the musicians doggedly play the song with a horribly discordant bent note from Belew's Dwayne Eddie-style lead guitar, ensuring we know the song is meant to be about an unpleasant experience. Bowie repeated this trick on the shocking title track of his penultimate album *The Next Day* (2013). It's like a horror movie in sound.

'Red Money' (Bowie)
We are here treated to a song with 'red' in the title (like 'Red Sails'), though it's less likely that the subject is China or even the East. Instead, this is about

big business. An alternative title could've been 'Blood Money'. The song describes cities, the loss of identity – 'Can you feel it in the way that a man is not a man?' – the alienation that comes with multi-national corporations and large organisations. It's also a warning of the destruction that will occur if big business is allowed free reign to despoil the Earth. Bowie sings, hopefully, 'Project cancelled'.

The rhythm has a stop/start, lurching quality like some lumbering beast, and sports one of those layered backing vocals, looking forward to the 'Let's Dance' introduction. The music is percussive and mechanical, with little room for much other than a grumbling bass line. The riveting verse-two lyrics have dark humour regarding 'a small black box'. Bowie's sense of panic as he desperately wants to get rid of this sinister device (is it a bomb, a flight recorder, a tracking device?) is hilarious: 'Stop it, take it away'. I'm sure this is what inspired Belew in the writing of 'Indiscipline' on King Crimson's *Discipline* (1981) since that also involved a mysterious device that caused consternation.

In some ways, Bowie's most mature album, *Lodger* ends with him telling us softly that the fate of the world 'is up to you and me'.

Scary Monsters (And Super Creeps) (1980)

Personnel:
David Bowie: vocals, backing vocals, guitar, keyboards, harmonica, saxophone
Carlos Alomar: lead and rhythm guitar
Robert Fripp: lead guitar
Roy Bittan: piano
Chuck Hammer: guitar synthesiser
Andy Clark: synthesiser
George Murray: bass
Dennis Davis: drums
Pete Townsend: guitar
Tony Visconti: acoustic guitar
Michi Hirota: vocals
Lynn Maitland, Chris Porter: backing vocals
Producer: Tony Visconti
Running time: 45:37
Studios: Power Station, New York; Good Earth, London
Release date: 12 September 1980
Label: RCA BOW LP2 (UK), AQL1-3647 (US)
Chart position: UK: 1, US: 12

In 1929, the Radio Corporation of America (RCA) purchased the Victor
Talking Machine Company and, later, in 1949, introduced the first of their
vinyl 45-rpm records. These began to take over the teenage market, with Elvis
Presley especially taking full advantage of the teen's love for the new singles.
Elvis Presley and David Bowie shared the same birthday – 8 January. Bowie
had been an Elvis fan, and after Presley, he was one of RCA's biggest-selling
artists. This was all to end after *Scary Monsters (And Super Creeps)*: Bowies
last RCA album. But as a rock star, Bowie had, to some extent, eclipsed his
old hero's cultural significance and could be seen as the new king of rock.
The marketing slogan for the album was 'Often copied, never equalled'.

Everything about *Scary Monsters* was a success – its singles (especially
'Fashion' and 'Ashes To Ashes'), its remarkable cover with Bowie appearing
in a distressed Poirot costume. Every track was conceived with great care,
even the video for 'Ashes To Ashes', being of great cultural significance.

Bowie was moving carefully and fitfully into new territory yet again. He
was partially riding the coattails of the punk movement but also making
inroads into the newly emerging new-romantic synthpop fraternity. In the
'Ashes To Ashes' video, he presented stars from the new movement as part
of his coterie, having trolled the underground clubs for likely candidates to
appear as extras in the film. Given heavy rotation on MTV at the time, the
video was post-apocalyptic surrealism central, using grainy altered images
with Bowie dressed as the Poirot character, being followed by an odd cast of
people under a black sky, and being menaced by a huge dump truck.

112

The music on this album had the feel of brinksmanship as if he wanted to challenge RCA not to release it. (The opening track was uncompromising stuff, with a woman screaming out the lyrics in Japanese). The tracks continued in the socially conscious vein of *"Heroes"* and *Lodger*, giving a frightening and alienated view of a world in which nuclear war still threatened and people starved whilst the rich and their multinational corporations self-evidently continued their depredatory activities in underdeveloped countries. The record was to be David's backhanded kiss-off to RCA, and he made sure that every word and every note counted.

'It's No Game (No. 1)' (Bowie)

Fired up by Fripp's angular and distorted lead guitar, Bowie laid into the international situation, describing the horrors of Western imperialism, third-world poverty and the indifference of politicians to the plight of the disenfranchised: 'People have their fingers broken/To be insulted by these fascists is so degrading'.

Bowie here used lyrics from an old *Hunky Dory*-period song called 'Tired Of My Life' (a diatribe on depression, which includes the telling line, 'Put a bullet in my brain and it makes all the papers'). But that lyric is only used in an extended version of this opening song at the end of the album – 'It's No Game (No. 2)' – which has a much more subdued vocal performance.

This first version is positively howled out by Bowie in a deranged manner, the words also at times virtually screamed after him by Michi Hirota: one of the two Japanese girls pictured on the cover of glam-rock band Sparks' 1974 album *Kimono My House*. Bowie wanted a harsh-sounding Japanese female voice, as he hoped to highlight the oppression of Japanese women: 'I wanted to break down a particular type of sexist attitude'.

'Up The Hill Backwards' (Bowie)

This is the first track I heard from the album when it was released as a single, and I remember thinking, 'What in the world is Bowie into now?'. The track is as nightmarish and depressing as its title suggests, with the music alternately dragging as it evokes the titular battle to ascend and then descending as if the song's protagonist suddenly takes a tumble. A vision of the punishment of the gods being visited upon us poor mortals, the lyric includes the morbid and damning lines: 'We're legally crippled/It's the death of love'. At only one or two points in the song, there is a let-up when a few screeds of Fripp's lead guitar give us surcease and when the tempo briefly increases between verses, with the interpolation of some unexpected Bo-diddley rhythms. The song is a quite unrelenting picture of a world gone wrong.

'Scary Monsters (And Super Creeps)' (Bowie)

This track is a lot of fun as Bowie chooses to sing it in his Mockney accent and somehow makes it seem like it's part of the screenplay for a dark TV crime drama: 'She 'ad an 'orror of rooms', he sings as if introducing a scene. It shares its subject matter with Elvis Costello's 'Watching The Detectives', which also deals with crime drama and its allure for the masses. He also manages to name-check Jimmy Page ('Jimmy's guitar sound, jealousy's scream') and then suggests that the protagonist of this song is the sort of likely lad that would tell you a shaggy dog story, while at the same time possibly being a serial killer or, at the very least, a stalker ('she asked for my love and I gave her a dangerous mind'), which gives us a good idea of David's dark sense of humour.

Tightly played and with a short, intricate guitar solo, this was another single from the album, though it was less successful than the others. Each line of the chorus has a beautifully bent note that leads into Bowie's 'Scary monsters and super creeps keep me running/running scared'.

'Ashes To Ashes' (Bowie)
No one could've predicted that Bowie would revive his Major Tom character from 'Space Oddity'. Even more surprisingly, despite its downbeat aura, the song was a big hit in the UK, even though it does have a beat which is syncopated and sinuous and a keyboard effect that seems preternaturally right. The album version is also punctuated with eerie moans that remind us that all is not well in the world of Major Tom.

What is the lyric about? There is no doubt that Bowie is again exploring alienation, with a particular eye on the apocalyptic. 'The planet is glowing' is somehow particularly discomforting in this context, implying the whole world had become radioactive, perhaps. But the most telling phrase is 'The little green wheels are following me', which is likely a reference to his early hobby horse, the UFO phenomenon, though even more telling is the line 'One flash of light but no smoking pistol', as it's the lack of supposed physical evidence to which disbelievers of Ufology most refer.

However, it was claimed by producer Tony Visconti that Bowie was remembering a tea trolley that was brought around the studios when he was recording at the BBC, which had 'little green wheels', making the line a reference to the mundanity of day-to-day life intruding upon the existence of the effete artiste. It reminded him that drugs would allow him to escape from boredom as he finds it difficult to 'stay clean tonight'. This is misleading, of course, as he is clearly disingenuous when he sings, 'We know Major Tom's a junkie'. At this point, Bowie was trying very hard to 'stay clean.'

'Fashion' (Bowie)
The song has a curious sashaying beat, allowing us to picture a model on the catwalk, showing off the latest gown or parading it around a dancefloor. There is a sense of unease about Robert Fripp's lead guitar in this song as if he's unsure if Bowie is sending up the whole fashion business or creating an anthem to celebrate it. The song is clever in this way, seeming ambiguous

114

and difficult to pin down, allowing a superficial hearing to give listeners who follow fashion some hope that this is just a fun song about clothes and culture. It's definitely an attempt at satire, though, with Bowie purporting to be a fickle fan of fashion: 'They do it over there, but they don't do it here', he sings disparagingly. However, the narrator is essentially criticising the trends of the fashion industry whilst poking fun at people's slavish following of it: 'Turn to the left/Turn to the right'. Taking potshots at the Fashion industry is a bit two-faced of Bowie, though, as he was always a doyen of the scene himself and kept a sharp eye on what was currently cute in the world of *haute couture*.

'Teenage Wildlife' (Bowie)

This is possibly the central masterpiece of Bowie's career. It's epic, nuanced, and broken into several sections that lend the song a symphonic aura. Roy Bittan's keyboard-playing gives it tremendous pathos and the feel of one of Bruce Springsteen's doomed tragedies, like 'Jungleland' or 'New York City Serenade'. In an online review for *Stereogum* magazine, Ryan Lees refers to it as 'what might be Bowie's most iconic song' and 'the album's towering centrepiece'. Bowie expert Chris O'Leary, writing in *The Guardian*, says it is 'a phenomenal owning of the future, it's still electrifying to hear today.' Bowie himself said he would 'give you two 'Modern Love's for it any day' (referring to his later hit from the *Let's Dance* album). He also said, 'I definitely set out to write an archetype, yeah. I've always been impressed with that kind of song ... I guess it would be addressed to my mythical teenage brother.' In notes written at the time, which he used as inspiration for the lyrics, he wrote, 'There's going to be a war... there's going to be chaos ... you're not gonna turn away....' It was as if youth and the threat of war really weighed heavily on him at the time.

It begins with the most fluid and liberated lead guitar from Robert Fripp, which he embellishes with increasing beauty and poignancy throughout one of the most extraordinarily inventive and sustained extemporisations of his career.

The song works on many levels. At the centre is the idea of a hunting season, when wealthy individuals come together to shoot captive wildlife on their estates. The idea of being hunted is, therefore, central to the song. On a second level, there is the idea of young people and teenagers, who are often the cannon fodder of governments and military regimes during wartime for reasons they may not fully understand. Essentially, this is an extended metaphor. Teenagers and young people, in general, are seen as rounded up to be given a gun and sent to the front. On a third level, there's the artist himself – the star, being hounded by paparazzi and press, and though that's the most superficial reading of the lyric, it's a subject David had much experience with. At one point, there's a memorable conversation where the narrator, harassed and seemingly distracted, says:

They say, 'David, whatever shall I do?'
They wait for me in hallways?
I say 'Don't ask me, I don't know any hallways'

The words are at once humorous and panicky, allowing the listener a
sense of how it feels to be 'the hunted one'. The section concludes with the
exasperating lines: 'But they move in numbers and they've got me cornered/I
feel like a group of one'. This not only alludes to Bowie's supposed chameleon
nature – his persona seemingly all things to all men – but it also leaves him
totally frustrated: 'Oh no/I'm not some piece of teenage wildlife'. Some critics
make much of his supposed rivalry with other pop stars from the new romantic
scene at the time, but I think he actually felt that they, like him, were only
more cannon fodder and more teenage wildlife for the paparazzi to chase.
Mention of 'the midwives to history' who 'put on their bloody robes' is surely a
reference to politicians who make those fateful decisions to send soldiers into
battle, knowing the great loss of life that will occur.

The lead vocal runs the gamut of affectation, using not only his natural
sound but many other types of vocal ticks and oddities. He's not only
utilising his mock-operatic ballad voice but also a very vulnerable, hysterical
voice that was already part of his vocal arsenal and the more-measured voice
of the journeyman rock singer.

In early 1980, when the album was recorded, Bowie was offered the part
of The Elephant Man in the stage version of the David Lynch film (about
the terribly disfigured John Merrick in Victorian London). As part of his
preparation for the role, Bowie was at pains to develop vocal strategies to
suggest Merrick's voice: a strained, almost lisping sound due to his facial
malformation. Some sections of 'Teenage Wildlife' were likely influenced by
these attempts at the voice of Merrick. The play was a success on Broadway
later in the year, bringing David many critical plaudits. He used no makeup
for the role, just his voice and his training in mime.

'Scream Like A Baby' (Bowie)

Based on the old song 'I Am A Laser' that was given to backing singer Ava
Cherry back in the days of *Young Americans*, this lyric was written to express
Bowie's hatred of modern society's authoritarian governments, despotic
regimes and their control over ordinary citizens. His voice is so committed
and full of extreme emotion. The music is a tight and delirious mixture of
hard-rock guitar and swirling keyboards nailed down by heavy bass, with
gloomy low backing vocals like a Greek chorus.

Connecting the song unmistakably with his 1975 hit single 'Fame', Bowie
uses a similar strange varispeed technique on the vocal as was used on that
song. Here, he takes us on another strange ride like the title track's TV drama
scenario, but this one is more of a gritty political thriller taking in mobsters
and their victims, drug cartels and one-way car rides. At the centre of the

song is the character Sam. We are led to believe that Sam is the best friend of the narrator, maybe a family member. We are led to have sympathy for his predicament: 'They came down hard on Sam'. Both the singer and Sam are at the mercy of the system. Whether that's a governmental system in the third world or maybe the mob is never made clear.

'Kingdom Come' (Verlaine)
Originally sung by Tom Verlaine, this is one of those effortless cover versions Bowie makes totally his own (like 'Criminal World' on the next album *Let's Dance*). So, in-keeping is this version with the other songs on *Scary Monsters* that most people may have assumed he'd written himself. It benefits from Bowie's wavering, faltering vocal, that vulnerable new voice he used: one of many in his arsenal of vocal curiosities. 'The face of doom was shining in my room', he croons. And there's that unsettling idea of something shining, possibly with radiation, since the whole song is an end-of-days scenario in which the captives will be freed and given pride of place in the new world order.

'Because You're Young' (Bowie)
Fine guitar playing from The Who's kingpin, Pete Townshend, elevates this song to greatness. No one would've been surprised if this was released as a single, as it almost begs for a 12" remix. 'I'll dance my life away', Bowie sings sadly, and it's clear he's washed his hands of human relationships for a while. The high Farfisa keyboard and roughly chopped chords give it just a touch of punk – part The Jam's 'Town Called Malice' and part Elvis Costello and the Attractions. It's another classic song.

'It's No Game (No. 2)' (Bowie)
Where the opening song was completely overwrought and disturbing with the extra emphasis of the Asian voice shouting the lines along with the lead vocal, this version of the song has more verses and is much calmer. Bowie sings in a resigned voice, and there's a more dogged, straight playing of the rhythm track as if this is the exhausted, wrung-out conclusion. It concludes with sound effects that suggest a sweatshop somewhere in the third world, a treadmill, perhaps in a place where the poor have to reinforce their hovels by 'putting camel shit on the wall'. It would be an understatement to say that this song showed a mature sense of engagement in the struggle of the oppressed, downtrodden and disenfranchised, along with Bowie's compassion for those less fortunate than himself.

Outtakes/Single/EP
'Alabama Song' (Brecht)
Previously covered by psychedelic rock band The Doors, this is given the full *Scary Monsters* treatment, with deadly chords falling like hammer blows.

It recounts the story of drunken men carousing as they try to escape their routine and deadening day-to-day lives. 'Show me the way to the next whiskey bar', 'Oh, don't ask why', the narrator emotionally tells us. And where Jim Morrison's vocal on The Doors' version was ebullient, Bowie's voice is resigned and down-beaten. His interest in the song may have stemmed from his time in Berlin, but having had a long interest in Germanic culture and art, it was a no-brainer for him to cover it. It was even released as a single.

'Crystal Japan' (Bowie)
Thankfully, this was included on the 1993 Rykodisc issue of the album. It's a stately, calming, otherworldly piece that takes us straight back to the alien worlds evoked on side two of *Low* but was written apparently as a soundtrack for a Japanese TV advertisement for Sake. That such a sweet, ethereal piece should arise from purely commercial need is a testament to David's virtuosity. His synth-playing, and especially the humorous amorphous bass sound, are to die for.

Baal (EP) (1982)

Personnel:
David Bowie: vocals, guitar
Tony Visconti: bass
Unknown session musicians
Producers: David Bowie, Tony Visconti
Release date: 13 February 1982
Studio: Hansa, Berlin
Length: 11:14
Label: RCA BOW 11 (UK), RCA Victor CPL1-4346 (US)
Chart position: UK: 29, US: did not chart

The *Baal* EP – available in the *A New Career In A New Town* box set – was released after *Scary Monsters* in conjunction with a televised BBC production of the 1918 Berthold Brecht play *Baal* in which Bowie starred as the title character. Though the production is difficult to enjoy, with split screens aplenty used by director Alan Clarke, the play describes Baal's dissolute path through life – a wandering minstrel in effect, with an amoral character, brawling and wenching from town to town. Baal is also a murderer and comes to a sticky end. Remarkably modern in its depiction of debauchery, the BBC production is both riotous and arcane: essentially an art-house movie for TV.

In some ways, Bowie's performance as the rakish poet is something of a dry run for the more cartoon-like goblin King he played in the 1986 Jim Henson movie *Labyrinth*: also a questionable figure. The music is archaic, certainly worlds away from his current sound and therefore not for everyone. However, it is impressive and well-produced by Visconti and Bowie, though in the end, something of a curate's egg. Bowie chose the play because he loved the free-spirited, though amoral, title role and truly felt some kinship with the roguish central figure. Perhaps it was a way to exorcise all his demons, depicting as it does the worst of human qualities; Brecht's point being that however awful Baal is, he merely acts out the desires of other men, who themselves keep such feelings hidden, sublimating their desires and hiding behind their middle-class respectability but secretly wishing they were Baal. In David's life, he had the elevated status in society that Baal seems to have in the play – as a minstrel poet, the groupies, temptation, fame, and the media clamouring for interviews: in some ways, the ultimate test of character.

'The Drowned Girl' (Brecht (Trans. Willet), Weill; Arr. Muldowney)
A song about a girl whom Baal has spurned, resulting in her suicide. It's somewhat reminiscent of the fate of Ophelia in Shakespeare's *Hamlet* and is the best of the EP's tracks. David's mellifluous acoustic guitar, complemented by a chamber orchestra arranged by Tony Visconti, is tasteful and does its best to give the song a decent setting. A video of this song can be found on the internet.

'Baal's Hymn' (Brecht (Trans. Willet), Weill, Muldowney)
This song attempts to establish Baal's amoral character. It was played solo in small segments in the original programme but is here sung with a devilish sneer. Bowie's mockney accent was never used to better effect. The ripe but rich accompaniment is quite a step up from how Bowie struck the brutal banjo chords on the TV version. There is also a prominent accordion and a small orchestra, beautifully scored by Visconti.

'Ballad Of The Adventurers' (Brecht (Trans. Willet))
This is the only song here that shows Baal in anything like a good light, as it's his lament for the death of his mother. However, he is basically a rotter, and for him, even the death of his mother is nothing more than confirmation of life's brutal nature. Sung simply, in the TV version, it was again an interrupted performance, with Baal sitting in the pub getting ready to murder his best friend in a jealous rage. The music is less ornate on this track but again backs this 100-year-old song adequately.

'Remembering Maria A' (Trad. adapted by Brecht (Trans. Willet), Servatius, Bruinier; Arr. Muldowney)
The least difficult of all the Baal songs, this one concerns Baal's reminiscence of a past conquest, where he sings that he can remember a cloud drifting overhead better than he can recall the face of a girl he loved. It is really beautifully sung by David and is his only moment of tenderness in the play.

'Dirty Song' (Brecht (Trans. Willet), Prestel; Arr. Muldowney)
The shortest song has Baal humiliating his lover Sophie in the TV version, simulating various sex acts with her, with a lyric basically boasting about his sexual proclivities. It's an unpleasant little number, with Bowie doing his best to impersonate a lecherous cad. The raucous oompah style brings this brutal show tune up to a very impressive standard musically, even though its subject matter again reflects the debased character of Baal.

Outtakes/Singles
'Under Pressure' (Bowie, Mercury, Taylor, Deacon, May)
Bowie was working on music at Mountain Studios in Montreux, Switzerland, when he found Queen, old friends of his 1970s protégés Mott The Hoople (Queen supported Mott on tour), also putting songs together there for their album *Hot Space*. In fact, Queen loved that studio so much that they bought the place, though Bowie simply used it because it was near to his Swiss home in Lausanne. Eventually, they decided to jam on something drummer Roger Taylor had initiated called 'Feel Like' and liked how it was developing, though they broke off to go for a meal in the middle of the jam. Needless to say, according to Brian May, when they got back into the studio, they'd forgotten exactly how it went, so Bowie grabbed bassist John Deacon's

guitar and reminded him of the seven-note riff. Luckily, Deacon took Bowie's intervention in good humour and they got going again, creating the song.

The song is mostly predicated on a kind of scat-singing by the operatically trained Freddie Mercury, who certainly leaves a mark on listeners with his lush earworm of nonsense and the emotional depth he puts into the lines he actually sings. Bowie seems transported enough by Mercury to put in an intense performance himself. In a 2008 *Mojo* interview, Queen guitarist Brian May said the two songwriters argued *fiercely* over the mix. But in the end, what they created was an all-time classic and a very unusual thing: a profound and affecting hit single reminding us that though we all feel under pressure in modern life, with its incessant media deluge of information excess, it is human relationships and love that give us a valuable sense of connection: 'Can't we give love one more chance'.

'Peace On Earth'/'Little Drummer Boy' (Fraser, Grossman, Khohan, Simeone, Davis, Onorati)

Invited to perform on crooner Bing Crosby's Christmas show on 11 September 1977, David was enthralled by the idea of such a respected old-school songster (original singer of that perfect seasonal song 'White Christmas') wanting to give a young songster like himself a chance to duet with him. Remembering his 1960s days with The Buzz and managers Ralph Horton and Ken Pitt when Bowie performed 'You'll Never Walk Alone' (and also sang the *Mary Poppins* song 'Chim Chim Cher-ee' at a BBC audition), he was hard-put to not accept. Was there still a longing to be accepted as a middle-of-the-road crooner himself? The result came out as a single in the Christmas season of 1982 (recorded in 1977) and reached 13 in the UK.

'Cat People (Putting Out Fire)' (Bowie, Moroder)

A suitably spooky and sinister single version of the song later re-recorded for the 1983 *Let's Dance* album; this is the original version, written for the soundtrack of the 1982 film *Cat People*. The recording doesn't have Moroder's better-known disco sound (he previously worked with Donna Summer) but successfully mines a rock rhythm. It was released as a single in March 1982, and it's interesting to wonder if recording this track began to give David ideas about producing an album with more of a dance music feel, maybe turning his attention to other producers who were experts in more of a disco/dance related area.

Live Albums

Only two of these live albums were released in the period 1964-1982: *David Live* (1974) and *Stage* (1978). The others are later releases of 1970s shows that Bowie sanctioned.

Bowie At The Beeb (1968-1972) (Released 2000)

Though not really a concert as such, these *Top Gear* sessions were recorded live in the Portland BBC Radio studios at a variety of performances between May 1968 and May 1972.

Only one of the first five tracks was released at the time: 'Silly Boy Blue' (from David's debut album). The other tracks – 'In The Heat Of The Morning', 'London Bye Ta-Ta' and 'Let Me Sleep Beside You' – were released on compilations later. A number of other rarities are represented as live performances, which were also released later as B-sides or elements of box sets – such as the *Hunky Dory* outtake 'Bombers' and 'Looking For A Friend' (one of the many songs demoed around the time of 'Space Oddity' and only released later in the box set *Conversation Piece*). Other oddities include a cover of Chuck Berry's 'Almost Grown' and The Velvet Underground's 'White Light/ White Heat' – a perennial live favourite of David's that he recorded in the studio in 1992, which was Mick Ronson's final performance on a Bowie record.

Santa Monica Auditorium Live (1972) (Released 1995)

David is at his best here, though the recording quality was rudimentary. The fire and fury of his backing band, The Spiders From Mars, are unstoppable; they are a powerhouse, with Bowie's voice like a flamethrower. Nothing can withstand the aural onslaught. First released as a bootleg in the 1980s, the gig was given a full authorised release in 1995 in Bowie's first box set of remastered original albums, *Five Years*.

Ziggy Stardust: The Motion Picture (1973) (Released 1983)

This is a superb document of Bowie's last concert as his alter ego Ziggy, though it's really only an adjunct to the film. It was remastered and – along with the film – extended in 2023 to include the guest performance of Jeff Beck, who plays on a couple of the encores – a medley of 'The Jean Genie' and The Beatles' 'Love Me Do', and Chuck Berry's 'Around And Around'. The Spiders are augmented here not only by Beck but by Ken Fordham on sax, Ben Wilshaw on flute, and David's old friends John 'Hutch' Hutchinson on guitar and Geoff 'Warren Peace' McCormack on backing vocals (who wrote an excellent memoir about his lifetime friendship with Bowie called *David Bowie: Rock 'N' Roll With Me*).

David Live (1974)

The album cover has been a talking point ever since its release and is at least as well-known as the music itself. It depicts David in a wraith-like, cadaverous, blue hue as if this wasn't a record of his *Diamond Dogs* tour with its post-apocalyptic Hunger City backdrop but the soundtrack to a zombie flick. The music is fantastically louche and erotically charged, with many of the songs performed better than they ever were in later live incarnations – although, the band were kept behind a barrier, similar to a pit orchestra. The album yielded a minor hit single with the Eddie Floyd cover 'Knock On Wood'. Later reissues have extra tracks, including 'Here Today': the opener of soul band The Ohio Players' 1969 debut album *Observations In Time*.

Live Nassau Colliseum (1976)
Originally released on the 30th-anniversary box set, this live album was eventually added to the *Who Can I Be Now?* box set in 2015. The performance is very studied, and the rhythm section of George Murray and Dennis Davis is honed to perfection. Each individual instrument is delineated with great care in the Harry Maslin mix. Bowie again revisits Lou Reed's 'Waiting for My Man', the apposite choice of song here, as David revealed many times in interviews that this period was the peak of his drug-taking excess. The music is extremely intense, perhaps at times even delirious, the musicians pushing the envelope and playing out of their skins, with 'Stay' given an extended guitar workout and *Station To Station* particularly sublime and exciting.

Stage (1979)
The first of Bowie's professionally staged tour documents. A good deal of film also survives from this era, and though it doesn't quite live up to the sub-Nazi Dr. Goebbels show of the 1976 *Thin White Duke* tour, it's still a fine band, including guitar wizardry from Adrian Belew and virtuoso violinist Simon House. Robert Fripp has said he was asked to tour with Bowie, but turned him down, as he'd just finished touring himself and needed time to recuperate. It's interesting to ponder how Fripp's strange and enigmatic style (he called it Frippertronics) might have embellished the songs. As it was, Belew used the guitar to create avant-garde art, making such tracks as 'Station To Station' his own. Bowie was extremely brave to open shows with gloomy instrumentals like 'Warszawa': the diametric opposite of a rock show opener.

Selected Box Sets/Compilations
Early On (1964-1966) (Released 1991, Rhino Records)
This compilation CD, already mentioned in the first chapter, was the source of David's early singles and is a great place to hear them and their B-sides (along with old demos) in one place as if it were an alternative first LP. Nothing beats hearing his first single 'Liza Jane' as if you were back in 1964 when the long hard slog to success first began for the bard of Brixton, with the newspaper-like cover and booklet taking you back in time.

The World Of David Bowie (1970)
This vinyl album was released by Bowie's original record company Decca (parent company for Deram, the label on the first album). The record compiles a number of tracks from his first album, with one or two important offcuts and rejected tracks. The importance of the album at the time was to show fans of 'Space Oddity' that Bowie had a deep mine of material from which fans might dredge up yet more hidden personas. The first album's Anthony Newley clone could now be seen in company with the mystic hippy Karma Man, the lowly mod newcomer-on-the-scene evidenced in 'The London Boys' (originally a B-side), and the voluptuary and sexual adventurer of 'Let Me Sleep Beside You' and 'In The Heat Of The Morning' (both rejected songs recorded magnificently with Tony Visconti after the first album flopped).

Images 1966-1967 (1973)
This compilation is similar to *The World Of David Bowie* but was released on the Deram label itself, with a cover seemingly aping the US cover of *The Man Who Sold The World*, having comic-book depictions of songs on the compilation. As such, it's a trawl through the back catalogue at a time when Bowie had hit the big time with 'Starman' and the whole Ziggy Stardust spectacle.

Now that it was expanded to a double album, it offered the whole of the fantastic first album with its quaint Victoriana and chamber-music settings, added the other songs already on *The World Of David Bowie*, along with 'The Laughing Gnome' (which Bowie was ribbed about all his life by the English music press), its more-beat-group-oriented B-side 'The Gospel According To Tony Day', and another B-side, the esoteric ragtime-flavoured romp 'Did You Ever Have A Dream?'.

The Deram Anthology 1966-1968 (Released 1997)
This later CD compilation attempted to corral even more unreleased material onto the market, including for the first time 'When I Live My Dream' (a song recorded by Bowie's folk group Feathers) and first-album outtake 'Ching-A-ling'. The single version of the debut album cut 'Sell Me A Coat' was also included, along with the demo of 'Space Oddity' recorded for the song and mime video produced by manager Kenn Pitt to showcase David's talents.

It's not a patch on the finished production by Gus Dudgeon, but it still has period charm. The rest of this compilation broadly follows the outline of the earlier vinyl album *Images*.

Conversation Piece (Recorded 1968-69) Box set (Released 2019)

This lovingly curated collection of demos and alternate studio takes shows Bowie's songwriting beginning to solidify into something more sellable, with a series of songs over five discs (originally released on the separate vinyl records *Spying Through A Keyhole*, *The Clareville Grove Demos* and *The Mercury Demos* for record store day 2019). It concludes with a newly remixed and resequenced version of the *Space Oddity* album.

Of the many tracks less familiar to fans and omitted from official releases, several stand out as great tracks in their own right or as revealing try-outs of later familiar songs. These are considered here as they will be of particular interest to listeners. All these songs are by Bowie unless otherwise stated.

Disc One
'April's Tooth Of Gold'

This is a quite unique little acoustic demo, with the same theme as the last of Bowie's flop singles 'I Dig Everything'. He sings of his appreciation of all life's little quirks, describing a list of acquaintances and friends who all have something interesting about them. But April – with her supposed 'tooth of gold' – is the least appreciated of these lovable characters. Like most of these demos, there is a certain confidence about the performance, with its strident rhythm and chopped guitar chords, making this a more enjoyable listen than many other artist's detritus left on the cutting room floor.

'The Reverent Raymond Brown (Attends The Garden Fate On Thachwick Green)'

This has a similar quaint small-town theme, revolving around the mundane activities of normal people, not a theme found much in David's songwriting. Only at this early stage did he focus much on the minutiae of everyday life. Here, the focus is on a Sunday school jumble sale in his invented English village Thatchwick Green. With references to the jealousies of the women's guild and the good Reverend who is 'noting down sin', this song wouldn't be out of place on the Kinks album *The Village Green Preservation Society*.

'Mother Grey'

This song has all the hallmarks of a Beckenham Arts Lab in-joke, with Mother Grey being an everywoman mother figure and the matriarch who upholds cleanliness in the home. All Bowie's friends and associates would have the same difficulties placating their parents whilst they chased fame and fortune, making a mess whilst their mums cleaned up behind them: 'Mother, mother, cleans the floor/Mother Grey', the backing vocals mocking her with their ironic 'broom broom'. A wailing harmonica gives the song a driving blues feel, twin guitars pushing the song ahead, though it was to languish in the vaults for decades.

'Goodbye 3d (Threepenny) Joe'

This is the only demo here that's actually quite moving, even as a stark acoustic recording. David goes a little beyond the previous observational lyrics, starting again with a description of everyday life, with himself and a girl going to see the performer Joe, whose description as 'threepenny' is a kind of implicit criticism and a reference to Berlin's *Threepenny Opera*: a Berthold Brecht play described as a social critique of the capitalist world. It's famous for the song 'Mack The Knife' sung at the beginning of the play, composed by Brecht and Kurt Weill (though based on a Medieval murder ballad).

Needless to say, Bowie was intent on bringing deeper lyrics to his songwriting, and when he conceived these songs, he always said he had a stage musical in mind. He was something of a hippy at this time and certainly enjoyed aligning himself with Brecht's socialist vision with its jaundiced view of empires and capitalism.

The song is sung beautifully with the occasional vocal melisma in the chorus, underlining Bowie's strong ballad delivery and giving the song its aching pathos as he sings to the underappreciated Joe: 'Goodbye, but please don't come back again'.

'Love All Around'

This is a straightforward love song with a gentle fingerpicked acoustic guitar, simply describing the object of his affections 'with kitten eyes so green'. It could be a portrait of a real person – perhaps sometime lover and journalist Mary Finnegan, whom David lived with as a young folk singer in the days of the Arts Lab. Or it could be blues singer Dana Gillespie, whom Bowie was also involved with in the late-1960s. Even ex-wife Angie could be in the frame, as she was also on the scene at the time. It's not as melodically memorable as the other demos here, but it has a certain winsome beauty.

'Angel Angel Grubby Face'

This lyric is more the Bowie we have come to know and love, with its edgy portrayal of a doomed love affair. Again, he employs a rudimentary fingerpicking for its hesitant melody, and the lyric describes a sad assignation with its inevitable parting: 'The train is leaving soon'. City streets and factories are achingly evoked, but this is a melancholy lost-love song. It bears similarities to the early work of Roy Harper – a songwriter Bowie appreciated, using one of his songs on the album he produced for his backing band The Astronettes.

'Animal Farm'
Nothing more than a short chant, this eerily presages the *Diamond Dogs* album four years before its creation. Like that album with its song '1984', a George Orwell novel is the basis for this lyric (*Animal Farm*). With a spoken section about a 43-year-old woman whose life feels like a spent force – her existence becoming meaningless living on animal farm, the nine-to-five grind of the working life ruled by politicians and the media, the song feels like a track from The Beatles' contemporary *White Album*.

'Lover To The Dawn'
Two versions of this exist in this collection, and it is really the only of these tracks to have been further utilised, having been used as the verse parts of the *Space Oddity* album track 'Cygnet Committee'. Here, it's another love song, but with a more reflective and sensuous theme, the subject of the song being encouraged to be the singer's all-night raver. The first version is a home demo, but the later one is a studio demo with John 'Hutch' Hutchinson from Feathers. The gender of the central character, 'the thinker', is changed from a woman to a man in the released version.

'Life Is A Circus' (Bunn)
Opening with chords and fingerpicking almost identical to Leonard Cohen's 'Hey That's No Way To Say Goodbye', this song is actually the first of these demos not written by David (but by Roger Bunn of English folk group Djinn). It's very much in the Simon & Garfunkel style, and Hutch took the lead for some of the song. Bowie sings a silly, high, almost falsetto part like a demented choir boy. Also, the lyric is a little risible: 'Life is a circus, it's not a fair'. Interestingly, the arrangement seems to presage that of 'Space Oddity' with its call-and-answer voices. A second version on the same disc only strengthens those similarities.

'Jerusalem'
This is not the famous hymn with lyrics by poet William Blake, but it's certainly titled thus with a nod to that great man buried in Bowie's London birthplace of Bunhill Fields. This is even closer to the storied lyric style of David's later world-renowned personas. With a dash of Dylan-esque surrealism, it's an all-out attack on The Man – that hallowed figure of hatred for hippies; the unfocused ire of all flower children aimed at everything staid, boring and authoritarian: the church, politics and the military. Sung in the declamatory mode of Dylan's 'The Times They Are A-Changin'', had it appeared on any of Bowie's next three albums, it would not have seemed out of place.

'Hole In The Ground'
No longer an unknown quantity, this song was re-recorded in 2000 with other older songs and released posthumously on the 2021 issue of the

Toy album. The simple riff comes out better in the later full-band electric version, but the lyric is not the most inspired, though its idea of people living in some subterranean lair is obviously one that generally inspired Bowie greatly, his instrumental *Subterraneans* later appearing on the *Low* album, and a professed knowledge of Bulmer-Lytton's novel about the people of a supposed underworld – ehe Vril-Ya – alluded to on *Hunky Dory*.

'I'm Not Quite'
This is almost identical to 'Letter to Hermione' on the *Space Oddity* album, and with twin acoustic guitars from Bowie and Hutch, it's as much of a treat as the eventual fully produced version. Hermione was possibly the only woman directly named in one of David's songs and giving her this distinction surely marks the end of their relationship as Bowie's first real heartbreak. After the song there's amusing chatter from David and John, acting as if they're putting on a show.

'Love Song' (Duncan)
Introduced by David as a song by 'a female songwriter who sings behind Dusty', the singer in question is Lesley Duncan, and the song, with its confessional lyric, has many similarities in style to those by Joni Mitchell. The fingerpicking is bolstered by simple descending chords; Hutch takes the lead vocal, with David producing a higher, ethereal backing vocal.

Divine Symmetry (1970-1971) Box set (Released 2022)
This is the second major box set. It advertises itself as 'an alt journey through *Hunky Dory*. Only seven songs amongst all the alternate and live pieces were unreleased and all appear on the first disc, so only disc one is covered here.

Disc One
'Tired Of My Life'
A simple acoustic demo, with lovely vocal backing, at times recalling the sadness and *ennui* of *Hunky Dory*'s 'Quicksand', with equally affecting results. 'You don't perceive, so I'm leading you away', David sings, but where is it he's taking the listener? Containing lines and a melody later used in the rather depressingly realistic opening and closing tracks of his first 1980s album *Scary Monsters*, this song likely has a more surreal and winsome destination with otherworldly connotations: 'Home where you've never been, non-returning'.

'How Lucky You Are (Miss Peculiar)'
I can't be the only fan who wishes this was fully fleshed out with a Mick Ronson arrangement. At times, it recalls the strange marching rhythms of

'Velvet Goldmine' – both songs aimed at a female protagonist (Miss Peculiar in this case) who has an inevitable allure for the singer with her 'shadow stalking'. The icy sustained piano of the verses clearly gives the impression this is a woman who is not as welcome a lover as she first appeared 'with the monkey on your back'.

'Looking For A Friend'
Also making an appearance on the live album *Bowie At The Beeb* and in the live portion of this box set, this is an undistinguished R&B-infused rocker with a sing-along chorus. The singer says he's 'wasted on the back step waiting for the phone to ring', possibly recalling a time when he waited in vain for a call from a record company willing to take him on. In a strange invocation of Major Tom (and possibly also Ziggy Stardust, who was soon to appear), he is also 'face to face with the spaceman on the wall'.

'King Of The City'
Beginning with acoustic guitar, eventually intertwining with some sweet lead guitar, and including several passages of strong backing vocals, this is a song about the singer and his girl 'finding their own way'. He is trying to lure his lover back after a separation, but it's hard to hold on to her when 'everyone is trying to be king of the city' – so many rivals in the pop world (not the least of which would've been David's old mucker Marc Bolan: the biggest glam-rock star in Britain at the time this was recorded).

'Right On Mother'
This song was apparently aimed at David's mother, who was present at Bowie's marriage to supermodel Iman in the 1990s. More likely, it's a fantasy representing his desperate hope that his mother would accept his bohemian lifestyle one day because she doesn't appear to have appreciated his choices and is said to have been less supportive of his musical inclinations than his father.

'Buzz The Fuzz'
This live track is presented complete within the context of a 1971 gig at The Friars, Aylesbury, England. It was written by Biff Rose. The last of the unknown tracks in this box set has a huge neon sign flashing the word 'hippy'. It tells the same tale of a woman who spikes the cop arresting her with LSD – the joke being that he loves the psychedelic experience and decides to 'turn on' the rest of the police force.

The Aylesbury Friars Gig is an absolutely fascinating document of Bowie *going electric*. He starts on acoustic with just Mick Ronson and then introduces pianist Tom Parker and the other Spiders From Mars, and they gamely try to keep up with him as he gets more and more inspired and animated. The gig was a famous bootleg long before it was included in this set.

Five Years (1969-1973) Box set (Released 2015)

The only remastered collection released during David's lifetime, this was put together with an eye on the general record-buying public, offering what was marketed as definitive overviews of whole sections of Bowie's career with a few added extras. This one contains the studio albums *David Bowie* (aka *Space Oddity*), *The Man Who Sold The World*, *The Rise And Fall Of Ziggy Stardust And The Spiders From Mars*, *Aladdin Sane* and *Pin Ups*. Though all the albums are (again) remastered, they tritely stick to only *released* material when creating discs compiling non-album singles, alternate versions or B-sides not included on actual albums. Here, the disc is called Re:Call 1. This means that the outtakes from previous CD releases – familiar and much-loved after their inclusion as bonus tracks on the 1990s Rykodisc reissues or on other attempts at career-spanning retrospectives such as *Sound And Vision* or *The Best Of David Bowie 1969/1974* – are predictably missing. These will no doubt reappear in future box sets purely made up of outtakes and demos, like the two listed here: *Divine Symmetry* and *Conversation Piece*. Instead, we get mono mixes, although the original version of later Spiders B-side 'Holy Holy' reveals why it wasn't a hit and hadn't ever been re-released: it is turgid and monolithic.

What makes this box set desirable is its beautiful presentation with the discs in replica miniature covers, bearing labels attempting to replicate the original vinyl – and the attendant live albums (in this case, the 1972 Santa Monica show (formerly a bootleg) and the soundtrack to *Ziggy Stardust: The Motion Picture*: the last performance by the band, in 1973). There is also a different version of the entire *Ziggy Stardust* album, remixed by its producer Ken Scott. With a booklet and notes on the albums by Ken Scott and Tony Visconti and a short foreword by Ray Davies of The Kinks, it is a desirable object.

Rock 'N' Roll Star (Recorded 1971-72) Box set (Released 2024)

Sadly for Bowie aficionados, this set only contains two songs never heard before, both of which are considered below. The 29 tracks that are 'unreleased' are only demos, outtakes and live versions of songs already in Bowie's back catalogue. The first five discs on the album contain a slew of early demos sketching out the first ideas for the Ziggy Stardust album, some of which were discarded, such as 'Sweet Head' and 'Looking For A Friend'. There are live sessions from radio & TV performances, including his two favoured Lou Reed/Velvet Underground songs, 'Waiting For The Man' and 'White Light/White Heat', and outtakes/alternative versions and variant mixes. An early band version of deep cut 'Shadow Man' reveals why it was discarded, as it does not work as a guitar arrangement and awaits the lush piano accompaniment of the later *Toy* version recorded at the turn of the millennium.

The final disc is a Blu-ray with 5.1 audio mixes and the original album mix, as well as single mixes plus outtakes and alternative versions. Included on the Blu-ray is an alternative Ziggy album titled 'Waiting In The Sky (Before

The Starman Came To Earth)' with an earlier track list of the Ziggy album, including songs like 'Velvet Goldmine' and 'Holy Holy', which were eventually shunted onto B-Sides of his singles. It is a curio that was also released as a vinyl LP for Record Store Day in 2024.

'So Long 60s' (Bowie)

Recorded in a San Francisco Hotel Room (probably on a cassette), with a verse melody that was later used for the song 'Moonage Daydream', this is a heartfelt farewell to the era that gave us Dylan, The Beatles and Jimi Hendrix. Only a rudimentary acoustic guitar accompanies this field recording. Bowie is fully aware that he was stepping into the 1970s with its craziness and excess, warning himself to 'keep your eyes open wide'. But his spirituality is not to be left behind as he reminds himself to 'let the vision flow inside'.

The chorus, not part of the song when re-written as 'Moonage Daydream', is fantastic and declamatory, singling out Hendrix in particular: 'So Long, Jimi!' The song breaks down when Bowie attempts a falsetto that taxes his vocal cords.

'It's Gonna Rain Again' (Bowie)

A full band outtake from the Ziggy sessions, professionally recorded and pristine, this is the little jewel in the crown of this set. Though rather slight lyrically and with only an acoustic guitar rhythm, it has bubbly bass from Trevor Bolder and a propulsive Bo Diddley beat courtesy of Woody Woodmansy. It also gives Bowie a chance to luxuriate in a familiar Hunky Dory style arrangement; his voice relaxed and instinctive, he's 'full of cocaine' and in his 'easy chair', but later, he'll 'groove around the Market Square'.

He's a new man, the song seems to be saying, and he feels celebratory, but the problem is revealed in the chorus: 'Everybody says I look the same'. This leaves him a feeling that he still hasn't achieved everything he would like to: 'I think it's gonna rain again'. But the track ends with a little distinctive Bowie giggle – he knows he's on his way!

Who Can I Be Now? (1974-1976) Box set (Released 2016)

The second box set containing full albums from a specific era released only months after Bowie's tragic death, this guides us through the period after the Spiders split and when Bowie began to toy with soul and disco. First, there's a salutary remix of *Diamond Dogs* – the record that showcased him playing much of the guitar parts himself and delving into the sort of sci-fi dystopian soundscape that he was often drawn to. The album is in its original gatefold sleeve, with the creepy opening poem printed over a washed-out polluted cityscape in sepia to help you get into the mood.

The remixed *Young Americans* album shows David as he first seriously courted fame in America, a large part of the album being recorded in Philadelphia with soul musicians. The accompanying disc *The Gouster* is an early version of *Young Americans,* with some tracks replaced by songs not used on the parent record, such as 'Who Can I Be Now?' and 'It's Gonna Be Me'.

The final of the three studio albums from this period is *Station To Station,* with a new mix and the older 2010 Harry Maslin remix, which recreated the sound of the 1974 vinyl version. There are also two live albums – the seminal *David Live* (in two different mixes) and *Live: Nassau Coliseum '76,* which captures David in the prime of his Thin White Duke minimalist disco-funk phase. A disc of single edits and other oddities completes the set. Again, the presentation box, the gold CDs and the historical data in the booklet make this a fine addition to the Bowie catalogue, sanctioned by the man himself.

Changesonebowie (1976)
The first of a forest of Greatest Hits compilations, this was produced in 1976 as if it was the perfect encapsulation of his career, as it attempted to present the best of the pre-Berlin period hits in an easily digestible form for the non-fan. Only the alternate sax version of 'John, I'm Only Dancing' was there to lure true fans.

Chameleon (1979)
This hilariously titled hit collection was only released in Australia, and by this time, RCA had caught up with David's continuing list of hit singles, including tracks from all three of the Berlin-era albums. Bowie loathed the *chameleon-of-rock* tag and sent it up mercilessly in interviews, though it served well enough as a metaphor for his talent for changing direction much as Bob Dylan and Marc Bolan did, all of them trying new genres throughout their careers, as if for fun. Chameleons, of course, only change colour to blend in with the background: something none of these rock chameleons could ever have been accused of.

A New Career In A New Town (1977-1982) Box set (Released 2017)
The third box set of period albums is as well-thought-out and presented as the others, even if the outtakes from *"Heroes"* and *Low,* previously released on the Rykodisc reissues and the *All Saints* collected instrumentals CD, were nowhere to be found. Indeed, there was also the matter of an album of demos supposedly created with musician Paul Buckmaster, which contained music David wrote for the film *The Man Who Fell To Earth,* but it was nowhere to be seen. Instead, the four original studio albums *Low, "Heroes", Lodger* and *Scary Monsters (And Super Creeps)* appear in remastered form. Along with these and some singles and B-sides collected on a disc titled Re:Call 4, there are songs from the 1982 *Baal* EP. All of these tracks are carefully annotated in the booklet notes, and the package is fleshed out with two different versions of the live *Stage* album – one sequenced as performed on tour and the other replicating the original vinyl.

Rare (1982)

Finally, amongst the more exotic box sets considered here, there is this oddity, again offering unreleased or rare versions of songs, but nothing really remarkable. Although, in the early 1980s – still the days of vinyl – it might've seemed exciting if you were unaware of B-sides like 'Holy Holy', 'Velvet Goldmine' and 'Crystal Japan'. The German version of "Heroes" ('Helden') and the Italian version of 'Space Oddity' (the opening track, no less) are not much more than desultory anomalies.

Productions And Collaborations

Dana Gillespie – 'Andy Warhol' (1971)

In 1971, Bowie stepped in to try and improve the visibility of his ex-girlfriend Dana's pop profile by offering her this wonderful and humorous song, which he recorded for *Hunky Dory*. Though he did not produce the track himself, he and Mick Ronson were involved in the making of the album *Weren't Born A Man* (1973) and gave the song a very different reading to the one he recorded. Dana's was cold and remote, whereas David's was light and fun. Dana's version was released as a single in America.

Mott The Hoople – 'All The Young Dudes' (1972)

The story of David's involvement with the production of Mott's first successful album is bound up with this era-defining track, gifted to the band by Bowie. Though it became the anthemic glam rock classic of the 1970s, Bowie could not seem to nail a definitive version of it in the studio, using only his sleazy saxophone as its main embellishment. It took canny lead guitarist Mick Ralph's elegiac and timeless riff, as well as vocalist Ian Hunter's cajoling voice during the track's fade-out, to turn it into a chart hit. The whole thing worked both ways; Mott elevated Bowie's status by getting to number one, and in return, he had given them a great song, which reflected well on the man himself.

Lou Reed – Transformer (1972)

With this album, Bowie literally pulled Lou's fat out of the fire. His first album had bombed and none of The Velvet Underground's albums had been big sellers, though they became cult classics. Bowie held Lou's work in high esteem but was nervous about working with one of his heroes. However, he eventually took on the role because 'elements of what Lou was doing was unavoidably right for where music was going'.

This resulted in one of the most sublime albums of the glam era, with several hit singles being culled from the resulting production, including 'Viscious', 'Satellite Of Love' and, of course, the towering all-time classic 'Walk On The Wild Side'. Lou's dormant career was revived, and Bowie had again sparkled his sonic magic over the sound, always, of course, with help from his right-hand man Mick Ronson.

Mick Ronson – Slaughter On 10th Avenue (1972)

Although Bowie was not involved in the production of Ronson's first solo album, he provided two songs: 'Growing Up And I'm Fine' and 'Pleasure Man/Hey Ma Get Papa' (a co-write with Ronson and Scott Richardson). The first of these, 'Growing Up And I'm Fine', is similar in tone to Bruce Springsteen's song 'Growing Up', which Bowie produced a cover of during the sessions for his album *Pin Ups*. It is a piano-led number with sudden bursts of energy, catchy lyrics about 'growing pains', teenage confusion and paranoia: 'somebody's messed with my brain'. 'Pleasure Man/Hey Ma

Get Papa' has a distinctive Hendrix-influenced lead-guitar solo before the song segues from the opening 'Pleasure Man' segment into the 'Hey Ma Get Papa' closing section, with very precise bass playing from The Spiders' Trevor Bolder and their keyboard maestro Mike Garson. The song ends with impressive use of guitar effects as well as Bowie-esque backing vocals and sound effects, such as children's voices and party chatter.

Iggy And The Stooges – Raw Power (1973)
Bowie's first attempt at a post-production job was Iggy Pop's third LP with his band The Stooges – *Raw Power* was the perfect title for the album. The songs, even the ballads, pummel the listener with sheer force. Although Iggy's own attempt at production was completed, David was asked to assist with post-production and mixing the album. Whether by design or because David was ill-experienced in a studio role, the whole thing sounds a little over-egged – the instruments are quite distorted.

Fortunately, this does not spoil the album as the raucous charge of the guitars predicts punk rock three years before the term existed and surely helped Iggy to claim that much sought-after mantle – the godfather of punk. Later, The Clash, The Pistols, SFL and others would seek to emulate the visceral thrill of 'Gimme Danger', 'Your Pretty Face Is Going To Hell' and, especially, the crowning glory of Iggy's career 'Search And Destroy'.

Lulu – 'The Man Who Sold The World' b/w 'Watch That Man' (1974)
Bowie told Lulu he loved her voice and 'wanted to make a motherfucker of a record with her' in a hotel after one of his concerts. She was encouraged to smoke many cigarettes during the session, which produced the correct rich tone Bowie sought for her vocal. What really distinguishes the song in Lulu's version, though, is Bowie's saxophone part, which gives the song its delicious, lilting tone. The B-side has less to distinguish itself, as Lulu tackles the opening track from Aladdin Sane with gusto and gives it a more extroverted sound than Bowie's original. The single reached number three in the UK singles chart.

Iggy Pop – The Idiot (1977)
'Jimmy was an amazing lyricist,' Bowie commented to Duran Duran's Nick Rhodes, 'so much better than me!' This is what constantly drew David to Iggy (Jimmy Osterberg) and drove him to help the wayward rockstar get his career back on track. He spent time with him in Berlin as they both fought to kick drugs, producing, playing and co-writing all the songs on this, the first of their three studio albums together. Bowie would later produce his own versions of several of the songs from this and its successor *Lust For Life*.

Opening track 'Sister Midnight' would be cannibalised by David for the track 'Red Money' on his *Lodger* album, for which he wrote much more sinister and cryptic lyrics, though strangely, he chose to play a cover of 'Sister

Midnight' later in his career. With second track 'Nightclubbing', the album produces its first standout track: a synth-heavy song that conjures up the surprising mental image of Iggy and Bowie as zombies in a German disco. 'Funtime', the third song, is really not fun at all, with its robotic, metronomic beat. The lyrics have a cool detachment to them, as Iggy's enunciation implies that anything but fun is happening here. The closing track on side one, 'Baby', is doomy and describes a trip down the 'street of chance' where Iggy sings that the 'chance is slim or none'. Many of these songs do seem to dwell on what the two friends were going through or had been through during their past careers, with many references to drink and desultory casual hook-ups. The mood of the album is resolutely down.

   With 'China Girl', the closing track on the first side of the original album, we get the punky, nascent version of a song Bowie would later go on to make into a much smoother hit. Iggy's version has the dual distinction of his fiery, raw vocal performance and superb saxophone accompaniment from Bowie. This is followed on side two by 'Dum Dum Boys', a song with a simple chord sequence that has a spoken intro, in which Iggy quizzes someone else about where this or that friend has gone, each time receiving a reply that the person in question has done something stupid. The song is pretty basic and has a repetitively 'dumb' chorus of 'da da dum dum day.'

   After this, there is the saxophone-drenched 'Tiny Girls', which continues a theme in Iggy's songwriting at this time, describing his need to find new paramours, maybe groupies, to replace the current girlfriend who he's become bored with, who 'wants for this and she wants for that'. He sings as if he wants to regain some lost innocence, the style of the song like some old rock 'n' roll ballad from the 1950s, but innocence here is long gone. The closing track, 'Mass Production', is another standout track and the closest in some ways to the sound of Bowie's then-current album *Low*. As with many of the tracks on this album, David plays a number of instruments to produce a morass of sound: piano, synthesiser, xylophone and saxophone. The lyrics speak of repetition, ennui and factories belching smoke, the astrally spiralling saxophones and synths howling in pain.

Iggy Pop – Lust For Life (1977)

This second album, produced in the interim period between Bowie's work on his own albums *Low* and *"Heroes",* has somewhat less involvement from David as production duties are shared between the Bewlay Brothers (a reference to a Bowie song from *Hunky Dory,* which we can take to mean both Bowie and Iggy working together) and Colin Thurston.

   The track 'Lust For Life' has become another of Iggy's classic tracks and was used in the soundtrack for the film *Trainspotting*, giving the song another lease of life. It has a pounding, rhymical pulse, the drums and bass being the product of the two brothers Hunt and Tony Sales, who later went on to become the rhythm section for Bowie's 1990s grunge band Tin

Machine. There is a triumphalism about its lyrics ('I've won a million in prizes'), perhaps reflecting the result of Bowie's and Iggy's success in leaving Berlin and their past lives behind.

Another track, 'Some Weird Sin', seems to be written very much as a standard Iggy vehicle, with much rock riffing in the Stooges mode, maybe with a little more pop nous from Bowie.

The early version of 'Tonight', a song which later became a hit for David when he duetted with Tina Turner on his own version in 1984 on his album of the same name, opens with a ballad-style intro. This somehow hampers the song's natural ebullience, though it is still melodically strong.

With the song 'Success', there is Iggy's own take on the sentiments of Bowie's hit 'Fame', though with a lot more humour, 'Here comes Success … here comes my car … here comes my Chinese rug!' It is a diatribe about materialism with a churning rhythm. Then comes a long ballad with some great backing vocals from Bowie, though curiously, the album credits only have him playing piano.

The penultimate song, 'Neighbourhood Threat', is a murky and muddy production, especially in comparison to the later, reggae-fied version on David's 1984 album *Tonight*. Again, there are evocative backing vocals on the song, with David's voice clearly audible, helping to distinguish this version greatly. The album ends with a track called 'Fall In Love With Me', a song which mentions 'West Berlin' in its lyrics, setting the song in space and time like a fly caught in amber.

Both of the two Iggy Pop albums Bowie worked on have become accepted classics now and were very influential in their day, with the two being remastered in 2020 and containing liner notes by Siouxsie Sioux, Youth of Killing Joke, Nick Rhodes and Martin Gore of Depeche Mode, all of whom remember being much affected by them at the time.

Bowie's Favourites
David Bowie's 24 Favourite Albums (from Vanity Fair magazine)
The Last Poets – The Last Poets
The Fabulous Little Richard – Little Richard
Music For 18 Musicians – Steve Reich
The Velvet Underground & Nico – The Velvet Underground
Tupelo Blues – John Lee Hooker
Blues, Rags And Hollers – Koerner, Ray and Glover
The Apollo Theatre Presents: In Person! The James Brown Show – James Brown
Forces Of Victory – Linton Kwesi Johnson
The Red Flower Of Tachai Blossoms Everywhere: Music Played On National Instruments – Various Artists
Banana Moon – Daevid Allen
Jacques Brel Is Alive And Well And Living In Paris – Cast Album
The Electrosoniks: Electronic Music – Tom Dissevelt
The 5000 Spirits Of The Layers Of The Onion – The Incredible String Band
Ten Songs By Tucker Zimmerman – Tucker Zimmerman
Four Last Songs (Strauss) – Gundula Janowitz
The Ascension – Glenn Branca
The Madcap Laughs – Syd Barrett
Black Angels – George Crumb
Funky Kingston – Toots & The Maytals
Delusion Of The Fury – Harry Partch
Oh Yeah – Charles Mingus
Le Sacre Du Printemps – Igor Stravinsky
The Fugs – The Fugs
The Glory Of The Human Voice – Florence Foster Jenkins

Bowie's Favourite Singles
Listed in a 1979 radio interview – except the last, which comes from an article in *Vanity Fair* magazine, erroneously listed as one of his favourite albums.

1. The Doors – 'Love Street'
2. The Stooges – 'TV Eye'
3. John Lennon – 'Remember'
4. ? & The Mysterians – '96 Tears'
5. Philip Glass – 'Trial Prison' from *Einstein On The Beach*
6. Velvet Underground – 'Sweet Jane'
7. Mars – 'Helen Fordsdale'
8. Little Richard – 'Memphis Tennessee'
9. King Crimson – '21st Century Schizoid Man'
10. Talking Heads – 'Warning Sign'
11. Jeff Beck – 'Beck's Bolero'
12. Ronnie Spector – 'Try Some Buy Some'

13. T.REX – '20th Century Boy'
14. The Mekons – 'Where Were You'
15. Steve Forbert – 'Big City Cat'
16. The Rolling Stones – 'We Love You'
17. Roxy Music – '2HB'
18. Bruce Springsteen – 'It's Hard To Be A Saint In The City'
19. Stevie Wonder – 'Fingertips'
20. Blondie – 'Rip Her To Shreds'
21. Bob Seger – 'Beautiful Loser'
22. Talking Heads – 'The Book I Read'
23. Roxy Music – 'For Your Pleasure'
24. King Curtis – 'Something On Your Mind'
25. The Staple Singers – 'Tellin' Lies'
26. Robert Wyatt – 'Shipbuilding'

On Track Series
Allman Brothers Band – Andrew Wild 978-1-78952-252-5
Tori Amos – Lisa Torem 978-1-78952-142-9
Aphex Twin – Beau Waddell 978-1-78952-267-9
Asia – Peter Braidis 978-1-78952-099-6
Badfinger – Robert Day-Webb 978-1-878952-176-4
Barclay James Harvest – Keith And Monica Domone 978-1-78952-067-5
Beck – Arthur Lizie 978-1-78952-258-7
The Beatles – Andrew Wild 978-1-78952-009-5
The Beatles Solo 1969-1980 – Andrew Wild 978-1-78952-030-9
Blue Oyster Cult – Jacob Holm-Lupo 978-1-78952-007-1
Blur – Matt Bishop 978-178952-164-1
Marc Bolan And T.rex – Peter Gallagher 978-1-78952-124-5
Kate Bush – Bill Thomas 978-1-78952-097-2
Camel – Hamish Kuzminski 978-1-78952-040-8
Captain Beefheart – Opher Goodwin 978-1-78952-235-8
Caravan – Andy Boot 978-1-78952-127-6
Cardiacs – Eric Benac 978-1-78952-131-3
Nick Cave And The Bad Seeds – Dominic Sanderson 978-1-78952-240-2
Eric Clapton Solo – Andrew Wild 978-1-78952-141-2
The Clash – Nick Assirati 978-1-78952-077-4
Elvis Costello And The Attractions – Georg Purvis 978-1-78952-129-0
Crosby, Stills & Nash – Andrew Wild 978-1-78952-039-2
Creedence Clearwater Revival – Tony Thompson 978-178952-237-2
The Damned – Morgan Brown 978-1-78952-136-8
Deep Purple And Rainbow 1968-79 – Steve Pilkington 978-1-78952-002-6
Dire Straits – Andrew Wild 978-1-78952-044-6
The Doors – Tony Thompson 978-1-78952-137-5
Dream Theater – Jordan Blum 978-1-78952-050-7
Eagles – John Van Der Kiste 978-1-78952-260-0
Earth, Wind And Fire – Bud Wilkins 978-1-78952-272-3
Electric Light Orchestra – Barry Delve 978-1-78952-152-8
Emerson Lake And Palmer – Mike Goode 978-1-78952-000-2
Fairport Convention – Kevan Furbank 978-1-78952-051-4
Peter Gabriel – Graeme Scarfe 978-1-78952-138-2
Genesis – Stuart Macfarlane 978-1-78952-005-7
Gentle Giant – Gary Steel 978-1-78952-058-3
Gong – Kevan Furbank 978-1-78952-082-8
Green Day – William E. Spevack 978-1-78952-261-7
Hall And Oates – Ian Abrahams 978-1-78952-167-2
Hawkwind – Duncan Harris 978-1-78952-052-1
Peter Hammill – Richard Rees Jones 978-1-78952-163-4
Roy Harper – Opher Goodwin 978-1-78952-130-6

Jimi Hendrix – Emma Stott 978-1-78952-175-7
The Hollies – Andrew Darlington 978-1-78952-159-7
Horslips – Richard James 978-1-78952-263-1
The Human League And The Sheffield Scene –
Andrew Darlington 978-1-78952-186-3
The Incredible String Band – Tim Moon 978-1-78952-107-8
Iron Maiden – Steve Pilkington 978-1-78952-061-3
Joe Jackson – Richard James 978-1-78952-189-4
Jefferson Airplane – Richard Butterworth 978-1-78952-143-6
Jethro Tull – Jordan Blum 978-1-78952-016-3
Elton John In The 1970s – Peter Kearns 978-1-78952-034-7
Billy Joel – Lisa Torem 978-1-78952-183-2
Judas Priest – John Tucker 978-1-78952-018-7
Kansas – Kevin Cummings 978-1-78952-057-6
The Kinks – Martin Hutchinson 978-1-78952-172-6
Korn – Matt Karpe 978-1-78952-153-5
Led Zeppelin – Steve Pilkington 978-1-78952-151-1
Level 42 – Matt Philips 978-1-78952-102-3
Little Feat – Georg Purvis - 978-1-78952-168-9
Aimee Mann – Jez Rowden 978-1-78952-036-1
Joni Mitchell – Peter Kearns 978-1-78952-081-1
The Moody Blues – Geoffrey Feakes 978-1-78952-042-2
Motorhead – Duncan Harris 978-1-78952-173-3
Nektar – Scott Meze – 978-1-78952-257-0
New Order – Dennis Remmer – 978-1-78952-249-5
Nightwish – Simon Mcmurdo – 978-1-78952-270-9
Laura Nyro – Philip Ward 978-1-78952-182-5
Mike Oldfield – Ryan Yard 978-1-78952-060-6
Opeth – Jordan Blum 978-1-78-952-166-5
Pearl Jam – Ben L. Connor 978-1-78952-188-7
Tom Petty – Richard James 978-1-78952-128-3
Pink Floyd – Richard Butterworth 978-1-78952-242-6
The Police – Pete Braidis 978-1-78952-158-0
Porcupine Tree – Nick Holmes 978-1-78952-144-3
Queen – Andrew Wild 978-1-78952-003-3
Radiohead – William Allen 978-1-78952-149-8
Rancid – Paul Matts 989-1-78952-187-0
Renaissance – David Detmer 978-1-78952-062-0
Reo Speedwagon – Jim Romag 978-1-78952-262-4
The Rolling Stones 1963-80 – Steve Pilkington 978-1-78952-017-0
The Smiths And Morrissey – Tommy Gunnarsson 978-1-78952-140-5
Spirit – Rev. Keith A. Gordon – 978-1-78952- 248-8
Stackridge – Alan Draper 978-1-78952-232-7

Also available from Sonicbond

Status Quo The Frantic Four Years – Richard James 978-1-78952-160-3
Steely Dan – Jez Rowden 978-1-78952-043-9
Steve Hackett – Geoffrey Feakes 978-1-78952-098-9
Tears For Fears – Paul Clark - 978-178952-238-9
Thin Lizzy – Graeme Stroud 978-1-78952-064-4
Tool – Matt Karpe 978-1-78952-234-1
Toto – Jacob Holm-Lupo 978-1-78952-019-4
U2 – Eoghan Lyng 978-1-78952-078-1
Ufo – Richard James 978-1-78952-073-6
Van Der Graaf Generator – Dan Coffey 978-1-78952-031-6
Van Halen – Morgan Brown – 9781-78952-256-3
The Who – Geoffrey Feakes 978-1-78952-076-7
Roy Wood And The Move – James R Turner 978-1-78952-008-8
Yes – Stephen Lambe 978-1-78952-001-9
Frank Zappa 1966 To 1979 – Eric Benac 978-1-78952-033-0
Warren Zevon – Peter Gallagher 978-1-78952-170-2
10cc – Peter Kearns 978-1-78952-054-5

Decades Series
The Bee Gees In The 1960s – Andrew Mon Hughes Et Al 978-1-78952-148-1
The Bee Gees In The 1970s – Andrew Mon Hughes Et Al 978-1-78952-179-5
Black Sabbath In The 1970s – Chris Sutton 978-1-78952-171-9
Britpop – Peter Richard Adams And Matt Pooler 978-1-78952-169-6
Phil Collins In The 1980s – Andrew Wild 978-1-78952-185-6
Alice Cooper In The 1970s – Chris Sutton 978-1-78952-104-7
Alice Cooper In The 1980s – Chris Sutton 978-1-78952-259-4
Curved Air In The 1970s – Laura Shenton 978-1-78952-069-9
Donovan In The 1960s – Jeff Fitzgerald 978-1-78952-233-4
Bob Dylan In The 1980s – Don Klees 978-1-78952-157-3
Brian Eno In The 1970s – Gary Parsons 978-1-78952-239-6
Faith No More In The 1990s – Matt Karpe 978-1-78952-250-1
Fleetwood Mac In The 1970s – Andrew Wild 978-1-78952-105-4
Fleetwood Mac In The 1980s – Don Klees 978-178952-254-9
Focus In The 1970s – Stephen Lambe 978-1-78952-079-8
Free And Bad Company In The 1970s – John Van Der Kiste 978-1-78952-178-8
Genesis In The 1970s – Bill Thomas 978178952-146-7
George Harrison In The 1970s – Eoghan Lyng 978-1-78952-174-0
Kiss In The 1970s – Peter Gallagher 978-1-78952-246-4
Manfred Mann's Earth Band In The 1970s – John Van Der Kiste 978178952-243-3
Marillion In The 1980s – Nathaniel Webb 978-1-78952-065-1
Van Morrison In The 1970s – Peter Childs - 978-1-78952-241-9
Mott The Hoople And Ian Hunter In The 1970s –

John Van Der Kiste 978-1-78-952-162-7
Pink Floyd In The 1970s – Georg Purvis 978-1-78952-072-9
Suzi Quatro In The 1970s – Darren Johnson 978-1-78952-236-5
Queen In The 1970s – James Griffiths 978-1-78952-265-5
Roxy Music In The 1970s – Dave Thompson 978-1-78952-180-1
Slade In The 1970s – Darren Johnson 978-1-78952-268-6
Status Quo In The 1980s – Greg Harper 978-1-78952-244-0
Tangerine Dream In The 1970s – Stephen Palmer 978-1-78952-161-0
The Sweet In The 1970s – Darren Johnson 978-1-78952-139-9
Uriah Heep In The 1970s – Steve Pilkington 978-1-78952-103-0
Van Der Graaf Generator In The 1970s – Steve Pilkington 978-1-78952-245-7
Rick Wakeman In The 1970s – Geoffrey Feakes 978-1-78952-264-8
Yes In The 1980s – Stephen Lambe With David Watkinson 978-1-78952-125-2

On Screen Series
Carry On... – Stephen Lambe 978-1-78952-004-0
David Cronenberg – Patrick Chapman 978-1-78952-071-2
Doctor Who: The David Tennant Years – Jamie Hailstone 978-1-78952-066-8
James Bond – Andrew Wild 978-1-78952-010-1
Monty Python – Steve Pilkington 978-1-78952-047-7
Seinfeld Seasons 1 To 5 – Stephen Lambe 978-1-78952-012-5

Other Books
1967: A Year In Psychedelic Rock 978-1-78952-155-9
1970: A Year In Rock – John Van Der Kiste 978-1-78952-147-4
1973: The Golden Year Of Progressive Rock 978-1-78952-165-8
Babysitting A Band On The Rocks – G.d. Praetorius 978-1-78952-106-1
Eric Clapton Sessions – Andrew Wild 978-1-78952-177-1
Derek Taylor: For Your Radioactive Children –
Andrew Darlington 978-1-78952-038-5
The Golden Road: The Recording History Of The Grateful Dead – John Kilbride 978-1-78952-156-6
Iggy And The Stooges On Stage 1967-1974 – Per Nilsen 978-1-78952-101-6
Jon Anderson And The Warriors – The Road To Yes –
David Watkinson 978-1-78952-059-0
Magic: The David Paton Story – David Paton 978-1-78952-266-2
Misty: The Music Of Johnny Mathis – Jakob Baekgaard 978-1-78952-247-1
Nu Metal: A Definitive Guide – Matt Karpe 978-1-78952-063-7
Tommy Bolin: In And Out Of Deep Purple – Laura Shenton 978-1-78952-070-5
Maximum Darkness – Deke Leonard 978-1-78952-048-4
The Twang Dynasty – Deke Leonard 978-1-78952-049-1

And Many More To Come!

Would you like to write for Sonicbond Publishing?

At Sonicbond Publishing we are always on the look-out for authors, particularly for our two main series:

On Track. Mixing fact with in depth analysis, the On Track series examines the work of a particular musical artist or group. All genres are considered from easy listening and jazz to 60s soul to 90s pop, via rock and metal.

On Screen. This series looks at the world of film and television. Subjects considered include directors, actors and writers, as well as entire television and film series. As with the On Track series, we balance fact with analysis.

While professional writing experience would, of course, be an advantage the most important qualification is to have real enthusiasm and knowledge of your subject. First-time authors are welcomed, but the ability to write well in English is essential.

Sonicbond Publishing has distribution throughout Europe and North America, and all books are also published in E-book form. Authors will be paid a royalty based on sales of their book.

Further details are available from www.sonicbondpublishing.co.uk. To contact us, complete the contact form there or
email info@sonicbondpublishing.co.uk